MEN AND WOMEN
WHO MAKE
MUSIC

MEN AND WOMEN
WHO MAKE
MUSIC

———◆———

By

David Ewen

MERLIN PRESS, INC.: NEW YORK

Published 1949
By Merlin Press, Inc.

DESIGNER: MILTON J. GOODMAN

PRINTED IN THE UNITED STATES OF AMERICA
BY AMERICAN BOOK–STRATFORD PRESS, INC., NEW YORK

PREFACE

◇◇

I⊤ Hᴀs often been said that the musical interpreter is
the connecting link between great music and the audience.
Through the interpreter's virtuosity, through his scholarly
comprehension of the composer's intentions, through the
vibrancy of his personality and his power of re-creation, he
projects for the sensitive listener the aesthetic experiences
he has found in the masterpieces of music. Thus, the art
of the interpreter is as infinitely varied as the number of
interpreters: Each one brings to a work of art his indi-
vidual personality and background, which give it shape
and form and subtleties of expression. Thus, too, the art
of interpretation will always hold for the music lover a
singular and inexhaustible fascination.

This book portrays twenty-six great interpreters of music who enrich immeasurably the life of music lovers in
this country. With the exception of one, these interpreters
are, at the present time, the bone and marrow of musical
life in America. While it had been my original intention
to confine this book only to those interpreters who are
now actively engaged in concert work in this country, it
was unthinkable for me to prepare a book on virtuosos
which would omit an artist of the stature of Pablo Casals
(who has not visited this country for so many years, and
who is now in complete seclusion in Southern France).

v

The book makes no pretense at all-inclusiveness. Inevitably there are more than twenty-six artists who are integral parts of our concert experiences, who have deservedly earned the admiration and allegiance of our audiences. But because the interpretative art is so rich, it is impossible to include everybody of importance within the limits of a convenient-sized volume—impossible and, it should be added, undesirable, for the repetitiousness of the material would merely invite boredom.

I have therefore decided to include no more than twenty-six virtuosos (eleven singers, 7 pianists, 5 violinists, 2 'cellists, and 1 harmonica virtuoso), those twenty-six who might best represent a cross-section of present-day musical interpretation in this country; those twenty-six in whom the American concertgoer, radio and television enthusiast, and record collector might be most interested.

The present volume was originally published in 1939 under the same title and proved sufficiently popular to go into several printings. In 1945, extensively revised, it was republished. As the only book that throws illumination on the lives and personalities of the outstanding artists of the American concert scene, it seems to have acquired a place of its own. It was, consequently, decided to issue still another completely overhauled edition, again entirely reset. Six new chapters have been added, while the remainder of the book has been brought up-to-date, freshened and vitalized with new material.

The treatment in this book is similar to that adopted in a few of my other works. The attempt is to give the layman a more intimate understanding of the virtuoso art "from the point of view most easily assimilated and understood; that of the personalities themselves who have given shape and direction to music." (I am quoting from one of my earlier books.) The emphasis in this book is on "biographical and personal material: the biographical material enabling the reader to understand the background and circumstances which inspired the musician, and the personal material giving the reader an intimate introduction to those personalities that gave voice to this music. . . . Critical appraisal, however, is not sacrificed."

CONTENTS

◇◇

Preface   V

I. SINGERS

  1. *Kirsten Flagstad*   5

  2. *Helen Traubel*   22

  3. *Lauritz Melchior*   31

  4. *Lily Pons*   41

  5. *Ezio Pinza*   48

  6. *Lotte Lehmann*   54

  7. *Marjorie Lawrence*   67

  8. *Lawrence Tibbett*   73

  9. *Marian Anderson*   80

10. *Jan Peerce*   90

11. *John Charles Thomas*   96

II. PIANISTS

  1. *Vladimir Horowitz*   103

  2. *Artur Rubinstein*   110

  3. *Josef Hofmann*   116

CONTENTS

4. *Artur Schnabel*   129

5. *Alexander Brailowsky*   136

6. *Rudolf Serkin*   141

7. *Myra Hess*   146

III. VIOLINISTS

1. *Fritz Kreisler*   153

2. *Jascha Heifetz*   167

3. *Yehudi Menuhin*   179

4. *Nathan Milstein*   191

5. *Joseph Szigeti*   194

IV. 'CELLISTS

1. *Pablo Casals*   205

2. *Gregor Piatigorsky*   219

V. HARMONICA VIRTUOSO

Larry Adler   225

MEN AND WOMEN
WHO MAKE
MUSIC

I

SINGERS

◇◇

1. *Kirsten Flagstad*
2. *Helen Traubel*
3. *Lauritz Melchior*
4. *Lily Pons*
5. *Ezio Pinza*
6. *Lotte Lehmann*
7. *Marjorie Lawrence*
8. *Lawrence Tibbett*
9. *Marian Anderson*
10. *Jan Peerce*
11. *John Charles Thomas*

1

KIRSTEN FLAGSTAD

◇◇

I N T H E late 1930s it was said that there was taking
place in New York a rebirth of enthusiasm for the music
dramas of Richard Wagner. Between 1935 and 1940, Wagner was performed at the Metropolitan Opera House almost three times as often as any other composer, and almost always to sold-out houses. *Tristan und Isolde* alone
grossed $150,000 in nine performances, making it the big-
gest single hit that Broadway has known.

Yet to say that New York opera-lovers suddenly rediscovered Wagner would be to state only half a truth. It
would be more accurate to say that New York opera-lovers
rediscovered Wagner through the interpretative genius of
a new singer.

She came here unknown and unheralded; but after two
performances she became the greatest consistent box-office
attraction that the Metropolitan had had since Caruso.
Single-handed, this amazing new artist brought prosperity
back to the Metropolitan during some of the leanest financial years in its history. Even more formidable a feat, she
silenced forever those graybeards who, for years, have been
boring us with their reminiscences of Emmy Destinn,
Fremstad, and Nordica. There was no longer a need for
talking about the long-lost golden age of Wagnerian opera.

The golden age of Wagnerian opera was here again.

When captious remarks are made about the musical intelligence of opera audiences or about the discernment of music critics, it might be wise to recall the afternoon of February 2, 1935, at the Metropolitan Opera House. A new soprano, Kirsten Flagstad, had come from Scandinavia to make her début as Sieglinde in Wagner's *Die Walküre*. The number in that audience who, before then, had heard the name of Kirsten Flagstad were few. She had come to this country with no glamorous legends preceding her, no triumphant European reputation trailing her. The New York music critic, the late Oscar Thompson, had heard her sing in Oslo in 1932 and had spoken well of her, but his review had not attracted much serious attention. None in the audience at the Metropolitan that night, therefore, could suspect that she was above the usual run of perfunctory Wagnerian sopranos. Wagnerian sopranos do not generally, in one performance, emerge from oblivion to fame.

Yet she had not been on the stage more than a few minutes when the atmosphere in the opera house became electric. One could feel the tenseness in the air as though it were some physical substance. At the close of the first act, the audience rose to acclaim the new singer with a spontaneous outburst of enthusiasm, the sincerity of which could not be questioned. The presence of a great singer had been immediately recognized, even though she had come here unpublicized and unknown.

And the next morning. . . . "Mme. Flagstad is that *rara avis* in the Wagnerian woods—a singer with a voice, with looks, with youth," wrote Lawrence Gilman in the *Herald Tribune*. "The voice itself is both lovely and puissant. In its deep register it is movingly warm and rich and expressive, and yesterday it recalled to wistful Wagnerites the irrecoverable magic of Olive the Immortal. The upper voice is powerful and true and does not harden under stress. The singing that we heard yesterday is that of a musician with taste and brains and sensibility, with poetic and dramatic insight. . . . Yesterday was one of those rare occasions when the exigent Richard might have witnessed with happiness an embodiment of his Sieglinde. For this was a beautiful and illusive recreation, poignant and sensitive throughout, and crowned in its greater moments with an authentic exaltation."

Three days after her unforgettable début, the new singer appeared in *Tristan und Isolde*. For the first time in more than twenty-five years, Isolde emerged on the stage a glowing and vibrant figure, a human being swept by forces she herself could not understand, helplessly and inevitably succumbing to a passion which sucked her in like a vortex. Her voice—a supple and incomparably rich instrument—poured from her with facility and opulence.

An Isolde such as this had not been seen or heard on an opera stage since the golden days of Olive Fremstad. No wonder, then, that the audience that night felt that it had just rediscovered Wagner!

But for a fortuitous train of circumstances, Kirsten Flagstad might never have made her historic début in New York, and would have retired from opera before her art had achieved full enrichment.

Otto H. Kahn, on a visit to Oslo, heard her in *Tosca* in 1929 (not in 1927, as some reference books have it). He was so impressed by her voice that he urged the Metropolitan Opera Association to give her an audition. The Metropolitan immediately wrote to Flagstad asking for the details of her career. To Flagstad this inquiry appeared to be only so much routine on the part of a large opera house, and she did not take it seriously. Moreover, she found the task of translating her Norwegian notices too formidable a job. Finally, she was at the time seriously thinking of renouncing her artistic career for matrimony. She never answered the letter, and her name was momentarily forgotten by the Metropolitan.

In 1934, Eric Simon, the scout from the Metropolitan, heard her sing Sieglinde at Bayreuth and urged Gatti-Casazza and Artur Bodanzky, both then in Switzerland, to give her an audition. Flagstad was only slightly interested in the offer. To appear at the Metropolitan Opera House was, of course, a cherished goal; but she was already married and was more eager than ever to substitute a placid domestic existence for the strenuous life of an opera singer. Indeed, she had already confided to many of her associates that the end of the summer would bring the announcement of her permanent retirement. A few intimate friends, however, urged her to reconsider, and she agreed that the audition would decide the issue: a contract from the Metropolitan would determine the continuation of her career as a singer; refusal would mean permanent and irrevocable withdrawal from operatic work. Inwardly, she was certain that the Metropolitan would never accept her.

The audition took place in a small hotel room in St. Moritz. On her way to the hotel, Flagstad found a fifty-centime piece; that coin—which she has retained as one of her most precious mementos—warned her that good fortune was waiting. She was not nervous, nor uncertain of herself. She sang with full voice, cool and self-assured. But her true stature as an artist was not recognizable at that audition. The small room (which, in addition, was heavily carpeted) disguised the true quality of her singing. Besides, she was asked by Bodanzky to sing the Brünnhilde

Immolation music from *Götterdämmerung;* and, never having studied the part, she was forced to sing the music at sight. Both Bodanzky and Gatti-Casazza judged that she had a small and limited voice, hardly capable of coping with exacting Wagnerian rôles, but also that she sang with insight and intelligence. Then, only because the recent resignation of Frida Leider from the Metropolitan necessitated a hurried replacement, it was decided to give Flagstad a one-season trial in New York.

The officials of the Metropolitan did not even faintly suspect what a strategic *coup* they had made with Flagstad's engagement—still less that they had made an epochal discovery. At her first rehearsal at the Metropolitan—it was in *Götterdämmerung,* since no rehearsals were scheduled for *Die Walküre,* Flagstad's introductory vehicle—her golden voice (which she used, not *mezza voce,* as other singers did in rehearsal, but with full power) flooded the auditorium. Bodanzky put down his baton on the stand and listened, afraid to believe his ears. Paul Althouse was so stirred that he missed his cue. It seemed incredible—but there it was! An unknown singer from Scandinavia, who had made only a passable impression at her audition, had a vocal equipment and a stage presence which sent the memories of more than one person at that rehearsal scurrying back more than two decades to find a fitting comparison.

When it is recalled that Flagstad's first operatic performance outside of her native Norway did not take place until 1928, that her first Isolde (and her first performance in German) was not sung until 1932, and that her first appearance outside of Scandinavia took place as late as 1933, the comparative youth of her artistic career is emphasized fully. However, though Flagstad's career had been short

and unsensational before her Metropolitan début, it was
not lacking in essential and important vocal experience.

She came from a family of musicians. Her father was an
orchestral conductor, and her mother not only conducted
opera and operetta but coached so many experienced
singers that she was often referred to as "the musical
mamma of Norway." A musical heritage was passed on
from parents to children. One of the sons became an orchestral conductor, while another achieved a reputation
as a pianist. Their sister Karen Marie Flagstad Orkel was
for a long time a fine singer of operettas in Vienna. But it
was the eldest child, Kirsten, who made the name of Flagstad world-famous.

Born in Oslo on July 12, 1895, Kirsten Flagstad began
her musical education at an early age. She was taught the
rudiments of the piano, but showed no great aptitude for
the instrument. To harmony and counterpoint, or any
other theoretical aspect of music, she was sublimely in-
different. Such love for music as she possessed in early
childhood was revealed in her singing. At the age of six,
she could sing Schubert songs with a sensitive and refined
voice. When she was thirteen, she acquired a complete
vocal score of Wagner's *Lohengrin* and was so fascinated
by the music that she succeeded in committing to memory
the rôle of Elsa.

Flagstad's confirmation was celebrated by a party for
friends and relatives, during which she sang arias from
Lohengrin and *Aïda*. A friend of the family suggested to
her that her voice was too fragile for such exacting music,
that it might be ruined by abuse. To give her some direction in her singing, the friend offered to give her a few
lessons, and this was the first systematic instruction Flagstad received in singing.

She had, however, little idea of becoming a professional

singer. She was given a thorough academic education with the hope of preparing her for some career.

Flagstad then studied vocal music seriously for the first time, under Ellen Schytte-Jacobsen in Oslo. For three years she worked on her breathing and tone, practicing solfeggio assiduously, and making gradual but important progress. An extended period of study brought greater richness and texture to her voice, so much so that her teacher once told her that two more years of study would enable her to make concert appearances.

A performance of Eugen d'Albert's successful opera, *Tiefland,* was being organized in Oslo. Kirsten Flagstad's mother was at a rehearsal during which a candidate for the part of Nuri was heard and rejected. On her way home, Mme. Flagstad bought a copy of the vocal score and, giving it to her daughter, urged her to study the part. Two days later, Kirsten applied for the rôle. She was the eighteenth candidate, and was accepted.

Flagstad's début as an opera singer took place in her nineteenth year, on December 12, 1913. The impression she made—even though she was cast in a minor rôle—was so good that several important music patrons of Oslo combined to finance her continued study. One year later she made another public appearance as an opera singer, this time as Germaine in *The Chimes of Normandy.*

Her study continued first with Albert Westwang, and then for two and a half years under Gillis Brant in Stockholm. Emerging from this period of retirement and study, she returned to Oslo and made a successful appearance in Wilhelm Kienzl's *Evangelimann.*

In 1919, she was married for the first time—a marriage that ultimately terminated in divorce and that Flagstad never discusses. A year later a child was born. During her pregnancy her voice left her, and she thought that her career was over. But one day, after the child was born, her mother brought with her music from Lehár's *Zigeuner-liebe,* a performance of which was then being prepared in Oslo. Flagstad sang for her mother—and to the amazement of both, her voice had grown richer, more sensuous, and more beautiful.

She was offered, and accepted, a leading part in the Lehár operetta, and she was a great success. In 1921, Flagstad made an extensive concert tour. Then, returning to Oslo, she became a member of the Mayol Theater which specialized in the performance of operettas. For two years she appeared in the entire repertoire of great operettas; then, upon leaving the Mayol Theater, she became a member of the Casino Theater, to be featured in revues, musical comedies, and operettas. But she had not deserted opera. During these years, she also sang in thirty-eight different operas including Gluck's *Orfeo,* Gounod's *Faust,* and Bizet's *Carmen.*

Her versatility in singing light and serious music was curiously emphasized one evening in Oslo. She appeared at the Casino Theater singing a current American "hit"— *I Love You! I Love You!* (which she sang half in Norwegian and half in a curiously accented English); and on finishing this performance she rushed to a taxi and made for the local concert hall where she was scheduled to sing the soprano part in the Oslo Philharmonic performance of Beethoven's Ninth Symphony.

In 1927, Flagstad became a member of the Gothenburg Stora Theater, where she devoted herself entirely to the singing of great operatic music. She soon surpassed all her former triumphs in the field of light music and emphasized, perhaps for the first time, that she was a serious artist of prime importance.

Following a performance of *Lohengrin* in 1929, Flagstad was invited to a house-party of Henry Johansen, a wealthy Oslo music patron whom she had never before met. Friendship between the two developed instantaneously; all night they danced together. The next evening they met for a dinner appointment. The evening after that, they were engaged. Early in 1930, they were married —and from the moment Flagstad became Mrs. Johansen she talked of withdrawing permanently from her artistic occupation.

For a while, shortly after her marriage, she retired completely from her musical activities, with no intention of ever returning. But after several months, pressure was brought upon her to make a few scattered concert appearances. The Gothenburg Opera, which was having some difficulty with its casting, begged her to return for a few guest performances. In spite of herself, Flagstad drifted back to her career as a singer, then began to accept more and more assignments, and finally acquiesced in the fate which destined her to become one of the greatest operatic figures of her time.

Since the milestones in Flagstad's career before her Metropolitan début were not many, they can easily be pointed out. Her first German rôles were Elsa and Eva, sung in Norwegian. Isolde, the first rôle that she performed in German, was added to her repertoire in 1932.

Until 1933, her operatic experience was confined to Scandinavia. In that year, she was invited to an audition at Bayreuth. This audition, being successful, resulted in her appearance as Ortlinde and the Third Norn in the Ring drama of Wagner during the festival season of 1933. During her first period in Bayreuth, she continued exercising her voice and developing it, so that at the end of the season Intendant Tiejan of the Bayreuth Festival confessed to her that it was impossible to believe that it was the same voice he had heard at the audition. One summer later, Flagstad sang Sieglinde at Bayreuth.

And then the Metropolitan Opera House.

With her first season in New York, Kirsten Flagstad became the cornerstone of the Metropolitan repertory. During that first season, she sang the rôles of Sieglinde, Isolde, the Brünnhildes of *Walküre* and *Götterdämmerung* (both of which she was singing for the first time), and Kundry (also a new rôle for her, committed to memory by her in eighteen days!). When she sang, the house was sold out; and she sang often. Fortunately, she had been blessed with the stamina traditional among great Wagnerian singers. She sang Isolde and Kundry on two successive afternoons; Brünnhilde, Isolde, and Eva on three successive evenings— with never a visible sign of fatigue. Fortunately, too, she has never pampered her voice but, on the contrary, has always subjected it to rigorous exercise. When she practices, it is always with full voice. Even when she first studied the part of Isolde, which consumes about one hour and a quarter of singing time, she did not restrict the volume of her voice. A long and rigorous season at the Metropolitan, therefore—with several appearances each week—far from bringing any sign of weariness to her singing has, instead, brought it greater depth, intensity and power.

What an all-important place she acquired with the Metropolitan Opera House in her very first season was emphasized the following year. As a gesture of honor to its new star, the Metropolitan, for the first time in thirty-five years, inaugurated a new season with a German opera expressly to feature Flagstad. Queues, long absent from the Metropolitan, encircled the opera house eight hours before curtain time. And at the performance itself, the enthusiasm and outburst of acclaim that honored Flagstad was reminiscent of that age, considered permanently gone, when opera was the life blood of music-lovers in New York.

Flagstad's instantaneous success in New York is not difficult to explain. On the stage she is an imperial figure, dynamic and magnetizing. Her stage personality is such that it can even inflame the enthusiasm of a public that does not fully comprehend the greatness of her vocal art. I recall that when the motion picture, *The Big Broadcast of 1938*, was first introduced in New York, its featured stars—Martha Raye, Shep Fields, Tito Guizar, and W. C. Fields—went through their routines with only mild approbation from the audience; but Flagstad, singing the Brünnhilde war-cry from *Die Walküre* (music whose aesthetic implications are not easily understandable by the movie public) drew spontaneous outbursts of applause.

Her singing, of course, is a thing of endless glory. She has great power of voice, an extraordinary compass, and unusual flexibility. Her register is equally rich in both extremes, and she has a luscious *tessitura*. Her tones come freshly and easily, full of roundness and body, each tone attacked cleanly. The greatest dramatic effects in her singing are produced through the simplest of means: with a discreet use of falsetto she can voice a radiant ecstasy; with a carefully placed pause, she can dramatize an entire page of music; a subtle use of variety in her colors, and she can scorch a lyric line with the hot flame of her anger.

In her acting, as in her singing, she is most eloquent when simple. Her gestures are few, but they achieve dramatic effects that are poignant and profound. I recall two decades of Wagnerian sopranos attempting the expression of anguish—with the most elaborate wringing of hands and contortions of body—when, in the last act of *Die Walküre*, Wotan pronounces the expulsion from Valhalla.

Yet Flagstad with the simple gesture of turning her head slightly and permitting her eloquently mobile face to grow gray and soft has, once and for all, given expression to the grief and pain of Brünnhilde. In the same fashion, no hysterical motions of the body are required by Flagstad to speak the ecstasy of a woman in love (in the last scene of *Siegfried*) or the fury of a woman scorned (in the second act of *Götterdämmerung*)—only the contraction or relaxation of her muscles, the softness or hardness of her supple and expressive body.

Flagstad is not, off the stage, an unusually beautiful woman, though her appeal is unquestioned. Yet, like every truly great actress, she has the capacity of making herself suggest a vision of sheer beauty when the drama demands it. With the play of a smile at the corner of her lips, the erect carriage of a regal figure, the electricity of her eyes, she seems indeed—when Siegfried inspires her with love—a goddess become woman!

Flagstad's phenomenal success in New York aroused no little skepticism across the ocean. In 1936, she received an invitation to give several guest performances at Covent Garden, London. That England did not take this American discovery very seriously became apparent with Flagstad's first appearance. She sang Isolde on May 18, 1936, receiving a handsome response from the audience. From that moment on, Flagstad's popularity in London was almost as great as in America. The critics admitted they had been suspicious of her fame in America, but were now glad to acclaim her as a great artist.

In Vienna, where she appeared for the first time on September 2, 1936, her success was immediate. She had been engaged somewhat grudgingly. To some of the directors of the Vienna State Opera, the importation of a new Wagnerian soprano from New York to Vienna was strangely

reversing the tradition of several decades. ("Anny Ko-
netzni," they said, "is good enough for us!") But pressure
was brought to bear on the recalcitrant directors, and Flagstad was invited. Once she emerged on the stage as Isolde,
her acceptance by the Viennese music public was whole-
hearted. "The stunning thing about this Isolde . . . is the
way she sings," wrote one critic in Vienna. "The tone is
wholly effortless, wholly 'forward,' wholly soaring, floating
from her mouth as easily as a leaf floats from a tree."

In April 1941, despite the fact that the world was afire
with war, Kirsten Flagstad decided to put an end to her
American glory and return to her native land. She wanted
to rejoin her husband as a devoted wife should. At that
time, momentous events were rocking the world. Norway
was occupied by the Nazi enemy. Flagstad's husband was
one of the country's most notorious Quislings; after the
war he was prosecuted for treason and was saved from a
traitor's fate by sudden death in prison. Flagstad's return
to her native land at such a time—a return, incidentally,
facilitated by the Nazi *chargé d'affaires* in Washington,
D.C.,—appeared to many like a sell-out to the enemy.

Consequently, when the war was over and Flagstad returned to this country to visit her daughter (who had
settled here permanently) and to resume her artistic career
where it had been interrupted in 1941, there were those
who could not forget the circumstances under which she
had left. Flagstad insisted that on that score her conscience
was clear. Once back in Norway, she said, she had never
been friendly to the Nazis; indeed, she had consistently
turned down their invitations to sing in public or over
the Nazi-controlled radio. But her arguments were dis-
counted by many. Walter Winchell denounced her vio-
lently in his broadcasts. The Metropolitan Opera Association refused to restore her to the company of singers.

The University of Minnesota turned her down flatly for its concert series, and so did several concert impresarios. Columbia Records would not consider her for a recording contract. The American Guild of Musicians unanimously passed a resolution denying her the restoration of full membership privileges.

When she made her first reappearance in Chicago, the hall was picketed by three hundred women headed by Mrs. Rheus Peerce, president of the Chicago unit of the Congress of American Women. "We owe it to the democratic women of Norway who died fighting the Nazis to protest Flagstad's appearance in the city," she said. In New York City, too, there were pickets, who chanted anti-Fascist and anti-Flagstad slogans. In Philadelphia stench bombs were released within the Academy of Music, while outside the hall a demonstration against the singer attracted five thousand participants.

There were some to raise their voices in defense of Flagstad. "Nothing could condone the intolerant, un-American character of what took place in Philadelphia," exclaimed the venerable Walter Damrosch who, then and there, offered to demonstrate further his faith in Flagstad's innocence by serving as her accompanist at her next recital. Immediately following Damrosch's lead, five prominent opera stars (Geraldine Farrar, Gladys Swarthout, Julius Huehn, Karin Branzell, and Paul Althouse) publicly defended Flagstad. "It is disgusting," said Mme. Farrar, "that the democratic process should be misused in an effort to destroy this great artist, who is also a great woman."

The bitter and vituperative arguments between those who accused Flagstad of treason, and those who defended her, could not however drown out one salient fact: Whatever else one might say about her, one could not deny that she was an even greater artist in 1947 than she had been in 1941. Virgil Thomson, the brilliant music critic of the New York *Herald Tribune,* attended the recital in Boston on April 6, 1947 in which Flagstad made her first American appearance in six years. He reported that she "sang like an angel. . . . Never in the writer's concertgoing lifetime . . . has there been available any other vocal artistry of such sumptuous natural acoustics, such perfect technical control and such sound musicianship."

If, as an intimate friend of Flagstad, you had spent much time with her while she was a member of the Metropolitan Opera Association, you would have challenged—and justifiably—the novels and moving pictures that surround a prima donna's life with glamour. For there was little glamour in Flagstad's daily routine. It was rigidly systematic. She rose early, awakened by her masseuse who put her body through a rigorous work-out. After a sparing breakfast—nothing more than grapefruit juice—Flagstad spent the rest of the morning in complete relaxation, if there was no rehearsal at the Metropolitan. She enjoyed a cocktail before lunch, preferably a dry Martini. If her favorite dishes were served, the main lunch course was either fish pudding with lobster sauce or broiled chicken.

The afternoons were spent in relaxation, or in rehearsal at the Metropolitan, or in private study of her rôles. The evenings on which there was no opera scheduled were spent quietly, sometimes alone with books, her correspondence, or knitting; sometimes in the company of a few friends. Flagstad almost never attended parties, elaborate functions, or night clubs. Gambling, or the imbibing of liquor in great quantities, bored her. If it was the evening of the opera, she rewarded herself with a half-bottle of champagne when the performance was over. Then she went to her hotel suite and spent a quiet hour playing solitaire—to permit, as she herself put it, the music of the evening to leave her consciousness completely.

In those pre-war years, her summer months of vacation were spent with her late husband, her daughter, and her three stepchildren on her beautiful estate at Kristiansand on the North Sea. Here her principal diversions were swimming and the care of the rock garden. Vocal exercises were rarely pursued; about the only serious singing in which Flagstad indulged during these vacation weeks was at four o'clock in the afternoon when she prefaced her husband's afternoon nap with one or two well-loved songs.

Sometimes there were holidays in the winter. Her difficult schedule was frequently interrupted in midwinter to give her a breathing spell. At such times she took extended skiing or hunting trips with her husband, doing the cooking herself. Her specialty was meatballs with mushrooms, but only because she didn't know how to cook anything else! Meatballs-and-mushrooms was therefore the exclusive fare of Flagstad and her husband during these winter expeditions.

As a friend you would have found her gracious and easy to get along with. She did not tax your friendship with volatile moods; on the contrary, she was remarkably equable of temperament, almost never yielding to those tempests traditionally ascribed to the prima donna. In her earlier years at the Metropolitan, she was pliable and even-tempered at rehearsals, capable of working hard, open to all suggestions and advice. (Unfortunately, her phenomenal success later brought on dictatorial attitudes, and no longer made her quite so easy to work with!) As in the opera house, so in her everyday life: her nerves were like steel, and she literally glowed with mental and physical health.

You would also have found her an essentially simple

and undemanding person. Her needs were few. She detested display or ornamentation of any kind. She disliked having servants or maids helping her with anything. She always did her own packing, answered her own correspondence, and attended to the details of dress herself. Even at the opera house, she refused any help in the application of make-up.

What she considers the two greatest events of her spectacular career in America before 1941 prove the simplicity of her character. These two do not include her American début, when she suddenly emerged from obscurity to world fame, or her first appearance in New York as Isolde when she was cheered by a rapturous audience. Her two unforgettable American experiences are made of other stuff. The first took place in Detroit, when her automobile was escorted by policemen on motorcycles, with shrieking sirens, from the General Motors broadcast to the railroad station; this incident thrilled her as had no triumph in the opera house. The other was at a flower show in New York, where they had named an amaryllis after her. "I was never quite so touched in my life," she said simply.

Her phenomenal fame in the opera house has thrown somewhat into the shade her equally successful career in the concert hall. She fulfills from fifty to sixty concert engagements each year, and visits almost all of the principal cities in this country. In song, her art is no less profound nor less moving than it is in opera, and she is now accepted by the world as one of the great living artists of song.

2

HELEN TRAUBEL

◇◇

THERE IS something magnificent about the quiet assurance with which Helen Traubel *knew* that she would become a great singer. There is also something equally magnificent about her refusal to allow anything to deflect her from her appointed destiny.

She could have had a contract with the Metropolitan Opera Association in 1926, when she was only twenty-three years old—thirteen years before she made her actual début there. But she knew that she was not yet ready for the supreme test, and she had the patience to bide her time. There was no hesitation in her refusal to audition for Gatti-Casazza; nor were there regrets when during the next eight years in place of the glamour of a Metropolitan Opera career she led the humdrum existence of a church singer.

A little less than ten years after she had turned down this Metropolitan offer, she refused a $10,000 a year contract with the National Broadcasting Company and a $15,000 a year contract with the Radio City Music Hall. She accepted the substitute of appalling poverty. Both assignments were detours from the goal she had set for herself. A person who feels she has a rendezvous with greatness is impatient with detours (however comfortable and well paved), preferring the more direct if bumpier route.

Even after she did sign the Metropolitan contract, she rejected the easier road for the surer one. Edward Johnson, the general manager, selected the rôle of Venus in *Tannhäuser* for her début, to which Traubel felt unsympathetic. She rejected the selection and substituted one of her own choice, Sieglinde in *Die Walküre*. Johnson was insistent on Venus; Traubel was equally inflexible. A violent explosion ensued, during which Traubel was ready to tear up her contract rather than appear in a less favorable role. Johnson finally yielded—he had met the immovable force and knew it. And the Sieglinde of Traubel was a success, as she knew it would be.

Her decision to turn down a Metropolitan Opera contract in 1926 took courage. But it took even stronger fiber to *accept* it in 1939. At that time, Kirsten Flagstad was at the height of her popularity, something of a cult. To be a Wagnerian soprano at the Metropolitan meant functioning in the shadow of Flagstad's Gargantuan success. Many a famous Wagnerian artist had been completely obscured by it. A new, unknown singer would be doomed to almost inevitable failure.

Traubel accepted the challenge stoically. She felt that she was ready, and she was confident of the outcome. The standards set by Flagstad did not terrify her; hers were equally high. Her only concern was to satisfy her own exacting and fastidious artistic criteria. If she did that, she would be satisfied. She could wait patiently for the public's recognition.

For two years, Flagstad and Traubel divided the leading Wagnerian soprano rôles between them, with Flagstad, of course, getting the more important engagements. Though the limelight of public adulation was flushed on Flagstad, there were some to notice the dignity and compelling power of the newcomer's performances. When, in 1941, Flagstad left the Metropolitan to return to Norway, Traubel proceeded—calmly and with complete self-assurance—to fill Flagstad's shoes. She did this with such competence and grace that not only was there no perceptible deterioration of artistic standards but, equally incredible, there was also no diminution of box-office receipts.

Flagstad vs. Traubel—the debate on the comparative greatness of these two Wagnerian sopranos will for a long time concern opera lovers. That there should be such a debate—that, indeed, it should be so closely contested—is, of course, the greatest possible tribute to Traubel. Flagstad's right to belong to that imperial group of Wagnerian sopranos that includes Fremstad, Nordica and Gadski cannot be disputed. To this hallowed company now comes an American singer who has never been to Bayreuth to assimilate Wagnerian traditions at the source, and who has never served an apprenticeship in smaller European opera houses.

It is not easy to decide between the two, even after studied deliberation. Both create characterizations of heroic proportions; both are magnetic personalities; both are consummate musicians; both have extraordinary voices. There are, however, subtle differences. Flagstad has the greater natural voice which is always completely at her command. But if Traubel's is a less perfect instrument, it is still capable of eloquence. It has amplitude, range, richness of texture, dynamic power. If Flagstad's singing is more brilliant and lustrous, Traubel's is warmer and more human. If Flagstad's interpretation has more grandeur and stateliness, Traubel's is more personal and intimate. Both artists stir you, each in her own way; with each you have derived a slightly different insight into the great Wagnerian characters they portray. Which one is the preferable performance is something each must decide for himself; or, preferably, allow it to remain undecided.

By 1947, Traubel had so completely established herself as the leading Wagnerian soprano in this country—if not in the entire world—that when Flagstad returned here after a six years' absence and made flirtatious overtures to the Metropolitan, she was rebuffed in no uncertain manner. It is true that Flagstad's questionable allegiance during the recent war made her *persona non grata* to many whom the Metropolitan did not wish to alienate. But an equally important consideration for the management was the fact that, by now, Traubel had become too great an artist, and too firmly established as a public favorite, to assume a secondary role to Flagstad; and Flagstad, they knew, is simply not the one to share the limelight equally with any other soprano.

Traubel accepts her position—that of a great singer, and a very successful one—with the charming casualness of one who knew all along that eventually it would be hers. She is inclined to regard it in the same matter-of-fact way that she does her good health or her happy marriage. She is a big, lovable girl whose infectious (and justly celebrated) laughter is a clue to her continually sunny nature. She is remarkably free of temperament, eccentricities, or inflated ego. She couldn't tell you what she earns (which is somewhere in the neighborhood of $250,000 a year) because she doesn't care very much. Simple, homespun, wholesome, she assumes no attitudes that are foreign to her personality, nor is she ever tempted to put on phony airs. Very little disturbs her placidity. As her husband put it so neatly: "Helen is so good-natured, you can't be sure whether she's stupid or lethargic."

The same lack of snobbery that makes it possible for her

to sing popular songs, to play boogie-woogie for her friends, or to indulge in rowdy burlesque on guest radio programs, is evident in her everyday living. At her summer place at Laguna Beach, California (a rather modest upstairs apartment of a two-family house) she does her own house-cleaning and cooking. The only outside help she accepts—and this, on the insistence of her husband—is a cleaning woman who comes to do the heavy work twice a week. She avoids help in the dressing room of the opera house as well, and is probably the only famous prima donna today at the Metropolitan who puts on her own make-up and costumes.

Her life during the winter season is well-ordered, and not particularly glamorous. She gets up early (usually at eight in the morning), works on her operatic rôles with a coach until about noon, eats lunch, takes a brief rest, then works for the rest of the afternoon on her concert repertory. On the evening of a performance, she eats an hour or so before leaving for the opera house. The performance over, she retires, without benefit of champagne parties, or visits to night clubs, or long and smoky gab-fests with friends.

She avoids crowds, night-life, the social whirl because her career is more important to her than so-called good times; and she knows that health is a prerequisite for good singing. She avoids them also because, truth to tell, her tastes go to simpler pleasures. When she wants an evening of entertainment, she goes to the movies—usually Western films. She is an avid baseball and football enthusiast, a lifelong rooter for the St. Louis Cardinals (who recently appointed her an honorary mascot). If it weren't for the fact that she screams with excitement at every close play to a point where her million-dollar throat is subjected to hoarseness, she would be at the ball park every free afternoon. In the summertime she goes in for swimming, and fishing barracuda and halibut.

She dresses smartly (clothes by Adrian) but always in simple, severe lines. She never indulges in expensive jewelry or elaborate knick-knacks. Her one idiosyncrasy (if you can call it that for one of her sex) is a passion for shopping; as periodically as the passing seasons she goes on a buying spree, and for days afterwards the trucks bring countless parcels to her Essex House apartment.

Her interests away from music are throwbacks to a happy childhood. Her father used to read her fairy tales; to this day she reads fairy tales in preference to any other form of literature. Her baseball fever was first contracted as a girl when her father took her to the St. Louis ball parks, where he had his own box. Her love for fishing was also acquired in girlhood at the side of her father.

From her father, Otto Traubel, Helen inherited her warm-hearted personality and her love for the simple, wholesome things of life. And from her mother—a talented singer who refused to go after a career—she acquired her voice, and her profound love for music.

Helen was born in the German section of St. Louis on June 16, 1903. Papa Traubel, the owner of a drugstore, believed that there was more to life than work. He thought nothing of leaving his business in mid-day to go off to the ball game or fishing or duck-shooting; and he thought even less of taking his children out of their classrooms to accompany him. He had a zest for living, and he wanted his children to acquire that zest. He built a miniature roller-skating rink in the attic of his home for Helen and her friends; he maintained open-house for them at his soda-fountain. He even gathered Helen and the children of the neighborhood for a game of baseball in a nearby sandlot. To Helen's childhood he brought a warm glow that makes her today look back to it with nostalgia—and gratitude.

She was born to sing. She sang continually—and well. Her neighbors and friends seemed to take it for granted that she would become a singer; and so did she. At thirteen (one year after her father died) she began studying voice with her first and only teacher, Mme. Vetta Kerst. Mme. Kerst, an excellent teacher, was a martinet who subjected her more talented pupils to severe discipline. There is no record of Helen's rebelling against the intensive work and the relentlessly severe regime to which her teacher subjected her. She just took it for granted that to be a great singer she had to work hard, and she accepted the arduous chores without complaint. When there were tears it was not because she was overworked but because she felt that her teacher was never satisfied with the results. "When I am completely satisfied with you," Mme. Kerst answered sharply, "you will not need me any longer." By the time she reached the third year of high school, Helen gave up all schoolwork to devote herself entirely to music. From nine to six, she was at her teacher's studio, studying, practising, memorizing, and coaching other pupils.

She made her début in her sixteenth year, as soloist with the St. Louis Symphony Orchestra. Two years after that she toured with that orchestra in the South. Her voice had by now developed opulently, and she used it with intelligence and taste. Some of her friends suggested that European study was now called for to put the necessary final touches on her training. But Helen ridiculed the idea. There was nothing Europe could give her that she could not get in this country, and better. The first time she left this country was in 1940, to sing in Canada.

In 1926, Rudolph Ganz, the conductor of the St. Louis Symphony Orchestra, invited her to appear as soloist under him at the Lewisohn Stadium in New York City. She sang the *Liebestod* and brought the audience to its feet. It was this performance that attracted the attention of Gatti-Casazza, who was ready to accept her for the Metropolitan Opera. But Traubel felt she still had much to learn. Instead she returned to St. Louis and for the next eight years worked in local churches and synagogues, and all the while kept on studying, working, preparing.

In 1934, Walter Damrosch visited St. Louis to conduct the Symphony Orchestra there in a Wagner program. Traubel was scheduled to appear as soloist. That an unknown local church singer should have been chosen to sing Wagner upset the genial maestro who exclaimed that Wagner was not music for an amateur. After the first rehearsal, he put down his baton and kissed the artist. "It is a disgrace," he said, "that a talent like yours should be hiding in neglect here."

He extracted from her the promise that when his new opera, *The Man Without a Country,* was performed by the Metropolitan Opera, that she would consent to sing the principal soprano rôle. She kept her promise and sang in the five performances that the new opera was given. It was as a result of this appearance that she was offered contracts by both the National Broadcasting Company and the Radio City Music Hall, both of which she declined because she still had to make intensive preparations for an opera career.

In 1938, Traubel married William Bass. (This was her second marriage. Her first, to a St. Louis automobile salesman, had taken place when she was only nineteen; it was an unhappy affair from the very first, and after a few months they decided to go their separate ways.) The next few years were the leanest ones in Traubel's life. They lived in a small two-room apartment in the shadow of

Carnegie Hall, in New York. Frequently there was not enough money to buy food; and even modest luxuries—such as an evening at a movies—were not often to be thought of. But dire deprivations did not seem to bring on any discouragement. Helen was happily married. Her art was developing to her fullest satisfaction. She was getting her teeth into the Wagnerian roles at last.

On October 8, 1939, she gave her début recital at New York's Town Hall—a recital which she bought at the sacrifice of many a meal and many a movie. It proved to be a sound investment. She sang magnificently, and the critics acclaimed her. "Miss Traubel's voice," wrote the critic of the New York *Times*, "is dramatic and opulent, produced with the ease of a solid technical foundation and the poise of maturity."

Immediately, offers came her way, offers that she could accept. On October 22, 1939 she appeared as soloist with the New York Philharmonic-Symphony Orchestra in an all-Wagner program conducted by John Barbirolli. Her singing brought down the house. "Seldom, whether in the concert room or in the theatre, is it one's privilege to witness so eminent an achievement in the *Götterdämmerung* finale," reported Pitts Sanborn. "Of paramount importance were Miss Traubel's voice and singing. The evenness, strength, and splendor of color that characterized the former had their counterpart in the grand design of her declamation and the appropriately wrought detail with which the outlines were stored."

The Metropolitan Opera now made a second effort to get her name on a permanent contract. This time she accepted. On December 28, 1939 she appeared as Sieglinde in *Die Walküre*, (Flagstad was Brünnhilde and Melchior, Siegmund). The critics again hailed her performance.

And they have been hailing her performances ever since.

3

LAURITZ MELCHIOR

◇◇◇

LAURITZ MELCHIOR began his artistic career as a second-rate baritone in Italian opera, but he brought it to its culmination as the greatest German tenor of our time.

This transition from one range of voice to another—and coincidentally from mediocrity to greatness—was effected through the astuteness of a woman, Mme. Charles Cahier, famous American contralto. On April 2, 1913, at the Copenhagen Royal Opera, Melchior made his début as Silvio in *Pagliacci*. Following several other operatic appearances he toured Sweden in concerts as Count Luna in *Il Trovatore*, with Mme. Cahier as prima donna.

It was during these appearances that Mme. Cahier—a musician of extraordinary discernment—noticed the unusually soft texture of Melchior's voice and the flexibility of his high tones. These vocal qualities led her to suspect that Melchior might have placed his voice in the wrong range, and that, consequently, he was not being heard to best advantage. She, therefore, suggested that he try to readjust his voice.

It was a serious decision that faced Melchior, for the attempt would involve the immediate abandonment of concert work and the return to several additional years of arduous vocal exercises. It also meant acquiring a com-

pletely new operatic repertoire. But Melchior had faith in
Mme. Cahier's judgment, and decided to follow her suggestion. That decision changed his artistic destiny—and
gave us our greatest Tristan and Siegfried since Jean de
Reszke.

A second chance influence took Melchior from Italian to
German opera. On October 8, 1918, he made his return
début, this time as Tannhäuser in Copenhagen. The début
had only a moderate success, and other engagements were
not plentiful. The following year a friend invited him to
London, where he was at once engaged as a soloist with
the Queen's Hall Orchestra, directed by Sir Henry J.
Wood. In the audience was the celebrated English novelist,
Hugh Walpole. Walpole, moved by a certain human quality in Melchior's voice, decided to make contact with the
singer and place at his disposal Walpole's influence, advice,
and financial assistance for the advancement of his career.
It was Walpole who urged Melchior to study the German
language and to essay the more important Wagnerian
tenor rôles.

Once again letting himself be led by good advice, Melchior left for Germany and became a student of Frau Anna
Bahr-Mildenburg, the celebrated Wagnerian soprano of
Bayreuth and Vienna. Under her tutelage, he received
stringent and rigorous training in Wagnerian traditions.
For months, hour after hour, he sang for her the rôle of
Siegmund, as she analyzed each phrase for him and tried
to instill in him a coherent conception of the rôle. Not
until she was completely satisfied with the results of her
comprehensive instruction did she permit Melchior to
make his Wagnerian début. This took place on May 14,
1924, in Covent Garden when he appeared as Siegmund
in *Die Walküre* with Bruno Walter conducting.

And what a dramatic début this was for the new Wagnerian heroic tenor! At that time Covent Garden was absorbed in a forthcoming production of Strauss' *Der Rosenkavalier*—so absorbed that it completely forgot that a new tenor was making his début in *Die Walküre*. Through negligence, the required rehearsals for Melchior were not called, so that at the last moment the directors were faced with the terrifying prospect of having a novice appear without benefit of a single rehearsal! Desperately, Bruno Walter cried that Melchior must not be permitted to appear, that a substitute must be called. At this late hour, however, no substitute was available. Resigned to disaster, Walter let Melchior sing—and, after the performance, rushed backstage and warmly congratulated the "novice." Without a single rehearsal, Melchior had made his début as Siegmund with the utmost confidence and poise!

Two months later, on July 23, 1924, Melchior appeared in Bayreuth for the first time, as Parsifal, with Dr. Karl Muck conducting.

His ascent to recognition was now swift. The Metropolitan Opera Association—its Wagnerian repertory burdened for many years by inadequate German tenors—was eagerly searching the European horizon for promising material. Melchior had shown enough promise to be engaged for the following season.

On the afternoon of February 17, 1926, Melchior walked for the first time onto the stage of the Metropolitan Opera House in the title rôle of *Tannhäuser*. It cannot be said that this first appearance at the Metropolitan Opera House was a historic triumph—it took place on the same day as the blatantly publicized début of an American soprano, Marion Talley. The newspapers had found in this Kansas City girl much grist for their journalistic mill, and exploited her to the hilt. Moreover, a carefully planned publicity campaign on the part of the Metropolitan itself had

helped to turn what might otherwise have been a humdrum début into an event of national importance. Months
before her appearance, Marion Talley's simple Midwestern
origin was converted by the press into a native American
singer's saga. News items poured from the presses about
her background and training. Her sudden emergence from
obscurity to fame was dramatized. A few days before her
début, the newspapers described the special delegation of
home-town folk that had come on from Kansas City to
attend the première of its native daughter; much was made
of the fact that Talley's father, a telegraph operator, would
send out to the world his impressions of his daughter's
début over a special wireless set rigged up backstage.

The limelight had been focused so strongly on the début
of the new American soprano from the Midwest that, inevitably, the introduction of a new German tenor that
same afternoon was almost ignored. Few of the first-string
critics of the New York papers were present to pass judgment on Melchior, and the afternoon went by without
drawing much praise—or even attention—for the new importation.

But even if the major critics had been present, it is
doubtful if they would have recognized in the Tannhäuser
of that afternoon the promise of greatness to come. That
afternoon Melchior's voice had a warm and pleasant
quality which set it apart from those of other German tenors of the Metropolitan—Rudolf Laubenthal or Kurt Tau-
cher, for example. But it appeared to be a limited voice at
best, which—though manipulated intelligently—was incapable of mastering the intricacies or meeting the exacting demands of Wagnerian style. Moreover, on the stage
Melchior moved somewhat stiffly and uneasily. The best
that could be said of his Tannhäuser that day was that it
was a mannered and self-conscious characterization.

Melchior's career in New York was not destined to be marked by a sudden flight to fame with one performance, or even with one season of performances. His art developed slowly—evolved, changed, grew, and then burst into full maturity during several seasons of uninterrupted singing on the Metropolitan stage. During these years, his voice strengthened and grew richer. Its fiber took on sensitivity and strength, pliancy and resilience. He acquired stage poise, learned how to make each gesture telling and effective with economy of movement. His interpretation of the great Wagnerian tenor rôles became integrated, drawn intelligently even in minute details, a complete and unified artistic conception. Gradually his art grew on the Metropolitan audiences until, almost without their being aware of when or how it happened, he seemed to them suddenly the long-awaited answer to the most pressing need of the Metropolitan Opera House: a German tenor who combined a magnificent voice with a stage presence commanding respect and admiration.

Lauritz Lebrecht Hommel Melchior was born in Copenhagen on March 20, 1890, the descendant of a long line of educators and clergymen, two of whom had been founders and leaders of the Melchior School for Boys, famous throughout all of Denmark. He was the youngest of six children, one of whom—his best-loved sister, Agnes—was born blind.

The family was left orphaned while Lauritz was an infant. The care of both the household and the children was entrusted to Froeken Kristine Jensen, who proved to be as industrious and solicitous a housekeeper as she was a genius in the art of cooking (she was the author of the famous Jensen cookbooks). She looked after the children —Lauritz particularly—with the solicitude of a mother.

Each morning she dressed Lauritz and prepared him for the Melchior School; each Sunday morning she personally conducted him to the English Church where he served as a choirboy. It was as a choirboy that he first attracted attention. The Danish Princess Alexandra—then Queen of England—visited Copenhagen and attended the English Church. She singled out Melchior for praise, patting his head and prophesying a great future for him.

His first important musical influence was the opera. His sister Agnes—being blind—was permitted to attend the Royal Opera regularly, seated in a special section under the stage reserved for blind students. Agnes had her brother accompany her to each performance. Wide-eyed, he watched the world of illusion unfold before him, as the music poured opulently into his ears. Those operas made an unforgettable impression on him. He could not banish the vivid scenes from his mind, nor forget the gorgeous music. Before long he began to tease his father: he wanted to study singing seriously—he wanted to become an opera singer.

Money was not plentiful in the Melchior household, and without money a thorough music education for Lauritz seemed impossible. However, Froeken Jensen, the housekeeper, whose successful cookbooks brought her a comfortable income, supplied the funds needed. In 1912 her money opened for Lauritz the doors of the Royal Opera House School, an apprentice school for the opera house, in which students were given training in every branch of the operatic and dramatic art. A year of study brought Melchior from the school to the opera company itself; he was chosen to take the place of a baritone who had left the company for Germany. Then the series of happy circumstances already described changed him from a baritone to a tenor and took him from the Italian repertory to the German.

His Metropolitan début was preceded, a year earlier, by another all-important event in Melchior's life. Maria Haaker, a well-known German movie star (often referred to as the Mary Pickford of Germany) made a parachute jump from a plane while filming a picture. The wind blew her off her course, and took her into the backyard of Melchior's house near Munich, almost into his very arms. The ensuing romance culminated in marriage on May 26, 1925. Shortly after their marriage, *"Kleinchen"* (as Melchior affectionately calls her) resigned from her motion-picture work to become her husband's secretary, business manager, and adviser. She has been offered several tempting contracts by Hollywood to return to the screen, but she remains firm in her decision to devote herself to ministering to the need and comfort of her celebrated husband.

Since his Metropolitan Opera House début of 1926, Melchior has made history as the greatest Wagnerian tenor of our time. He has sung the rôle of Tristan more than two hundred times (his foremost predecessor, Jean de Reszke, sang Tristan fewer than fifty times), in sixteen different opera houses and under twenty-two different conductors, including Toscanini. On February 22, 1935 the hundredth performance of his Siegfried was commemorated. In honor of this event, Melchior was presented with a sword, to be used in all future Siegfried performances, forged after an old Viking sword in the Metropolitan Museum of Art by Kenneth Lynch, a famous New York metal craftsman. The presentation was made on the stage of the Metropolitan Opera House after the performance, by George Beck, Danish consul-general, in the presence of Gatti-Casazza, manager of the Metropolitan, and the Honorable Fiorello H. LaGuardia, Mayor of New York.

In Siegfried, Melchior has found the rôle in which to unfold his personality most completely. Here, perhaps, lies the secret of the incomparable authenticity and richness of his characterization. Off the stage of the opera house, he is Siegfried to the life, a heroic figure standing six feet three in his stocking feet, two hundred and fifty pounds of muscle and sinew. The size of his collar is eighteen, and his shoes are size twelve. Yet, the impression he gives is not that of oversize but of prodigious strength.

"Kleinchen" has frequently described how Melchior— like Siegfried—enjoys walking through the woods and listening to the birds. And, like Siegfried again, he is capable of athletic action as well as quiet reverie. Melchior's favorite diversion (once again Siegfried to the life!) is hunting. Each year, when the opera season is over, he sets off on a long hunting expedition. The pelts of his victims become the skins he wears for his warrior rôles. He keeps an accurate and comprehensive log of every hunting trip, every killing he makes, every experience he encounters. As you look through this log you will learn that on one trip he and a company of friends shot 368 pheasants, wild boars, and other game, and that, more recently, he himself felled a six-hundred-pound bear in the Canadian shooting hide-out of Richard Crooks, the tenor. You would also learn that in 1935 he almost met death. He was hunting wild pigs in South America when, turning around in a brush, he confronted a panther rushing at him. It required coolness of head, sureness of trigger finger, and accuracy of aim to save him from certain annihilation. The skin of that panther was subsequently worn by Mrs. Melchior as a coat. More recently, he shot a mighty sixteen-hundred-pound American bison.

Seeking an apt word with which to describe Melchior, you inevitably come upon "expansiveness." As his phy-

Lauritz Melchior

sique is, so are his daily habits. Whatever he does is done on a Gargantuan scale. When he travels, it is with twenty-two trunks, and sometimes with five dogs. A meal for him is a prodigious feast including appetizer, soup, beefsteak, potatoes, vegetables, salad, dessert, coffee, a quart of burgundy, and a big Havana cigar. He drinks beer in vast quantities when his day of work is over. When he wishes to walk, it is frequently a twenty-five-mile hike. When he prepares a snack of *Smörgasbord* for his guests—a rite that he performs once a year on his birthday—it comprises no fewer than one hundred and fifty varieties of food. A bridge game in which he indulges becomes an all-night session.

Expansive, too, is the number of his diversions and pastimes. Hunting, fishing, hiking are some of his outdoor sports; indoors, he finds equal pleasure in playing bridge, boxing, cooking (his *spécialité de la maison* is an oxtail soup that takes him two days to prepare), mixing luscious "fruit-bowls," and modeling opera characters in almond paste which he sends to friends for Christmas. He is also a rabid collector of curiosities and stamps.

The character he has portrayed so felicitously in his successful motion-pictures and in his guest "spots" on the radio—the good-spirited fellow who boisterously enjoys a good joke even if perpetrated on himself, and who goes in for schoolboy pranks—is Melchior in the flesh as well. His generally good spirits and geniality are infectious. Highly typical is an episode of the Christmas season of 1944, thus reported in the New York *Herald Tribune:*

"Twenty-five kindergarten children enjoyed a Christmas party yesterday at the Children's Aid Society's Jones Memorial Center, at which candy and gifts were dispensed by a jovial six-foot-three Santa Claus. Then the children joined in singing

'Jingle Bells,' 'Silent Night,' and 'When Santa Claus Is Fast Asleep,' led by the tenor-voiced Santa, who had appeared the night before as Lohengrin at the Metropolitan Opera—Lauritz Melchior.''

One of his curious qualities is a strong vein of vanity. He derives a genuine thrill from appearing at social functions in full dress attire, with his many decorations suspended from his breast. Innumerable have been the honors bestowed upon him: the Knighthood of Denneborg, the Knighthood of Bulgaria, the Saxonian Order of Knights, and the French Legion of Honor. He has been appointed by the King of Denmark "Singer to the Danish Court." He has received the Silver Cross of Denmark and the *"Ingenio et Arti,"* which has been given to only three men—the leading actor, poet, and singer of the country. He has also received the Carl Eduard Medal, first class, from Saxe-Coburg-Gotha, for his outstanding service at Bayreuth.

Although not usually "touchy" or easily inflamed to anger, he is very sensitive about his name. To have it misspelled or mispronounced makes his eyes bulge and his face burn with uncontrolled fury. To his credit, he has the humor to laugh at his own weakness. For a long time he carried with him a printed card which he gave immediately to anyone who abused his name. It read:

> "There is a tenor big and jolly,
>   Who's hardly ever melancholy;
>   There's just one thing can raise his ire—
>   To have his name misspelled 'Melchoir';
>   Such carelessness will bring a roar
>   Of rage from Lauritz Melchior!"

4

LILY PONS

◇◇

I N A W O R L D in which streamlining is omnipresent, it is no surprise to find a svelte Lily Pons usurping the operatic spotlight. The ponderous and heavy-set prima donna of yesterday has, in our time, given way (for the most part) to figures that are trim and petite. Lily Pons, surely the most famous prima donna of our day, actually fulfills Hollywood specifications. She is slight of build, weighing about 104 pounds and standing five feet two. She looks like a miniature of herself. She is pert, attractive, as graceful in all her movements as a dancer, at all times radiating charm. Her dark eyes bring to her olive-skinned face an intriguing suggestion of Gallic gaiety; her face sparkles like a new coin. All this, and heaven too—the heaven of a voice that is, in the best traditions of an age of singing, now dead.

And still another difference distinguishes Pons from the operatic goddesses of old. There is no suggestion in her of the volatile moods, tempers, idiosyncrasies, shams, postures, passions, and egomania that used to be called "the artistic temperament" and were invariably associated with yesterday's prima donnas. Whim or mood has no place in Lily Pons' life. She is as methodical and as businesslike as a bank clerk; as hardworking as a factory hand; as foresighted and shrewd as an executive. Her road to success was paved with incomparable industry: she worked one hour a day for four months on the aria with which she made her Metropolitan Opera House audition. Even today, with success assured and permanent, she does not allow herself the luxury of self-indulgence. She works as assiduously on her new rôles as she used to work on the old ones. Because her work is so taxing and time-consuming, she insists upon a well-ordered life.

Her day belongs to her many duties as a great singer: engagements in concerts and operas; rehearsals; supervising her costumes; designing her own clothes; interviews; business conferences. Beyond all this, there is her fastidious and somewhat elaborate program of exercise and health hygiene which, she explains, is the secret of her vitality. One hour and a half each day, in half-hour periods, is devoted to deep-breathing exercises. Once a day she drinks *tisane*—verbena, essence of lemon, mint, sage, all prepared in an earthenware pot; she follows the drink with a hot bath and a cold shower in rapid succession. A daily nap of about an hour is another essential in her health program. She is also meticulous about her diet. She eats sparingly, usually vegetables, salads, and fruits, but rarely meats; she drinks a glass of water every half-hour.

Obviously, she likes order, system, careful planning. Obviously, too, in a life as busy as this, a capricious temperament would only invite chaos. Fortunately, Pons is even-tempered, usually gay in spirits, highly sociable, easy to get along with. Not that she is without her personal idiosyncrasies! She is an incurable collector of *objets d'art* —her home is cluttered with them. She also has an almost religious belief that the number 13 is lucky: She was born on the 13th: her house and automobile license are numbered 13; she wears a pendant with that number elaborately engraved on it. But surely she may be allowed such indulgences, in the face of her wholesome sanity and balance! There is an engaging unpretentiousness about her. She is as unassuming as a housewife. She dresses simply, and at her Connecticut home she will usually be found in informal slacks and sweater. She does not smoke, and refuses to touch any liquor (even wine). She almost never attends social functions, avoids night clubs like the plague, and is usually in bed well before midnight. Apart from the society of a few close friends, she guards her privacy jealously. She begrudges any outside intrusions upon her private life with her husband at their beautiful home in Silvermine, Connecticut, called Gentilhommerie.

Her husband is, of course, famous in his own right; his name—André Kostelanetz, the celebrated orchestra Maestro. They were married at Gentilhommerie on June 2, 1938, after a whirlwind courtship during which Kostelanetz proposed to her—yes, thirteen times—in person, by long-distance telephone, and by plane. Since then, they have become the most successful husband-and-wife act in serious music.

Her personal charm, as infectious on the stage as off it, her capacity to invest each of her rôles with an engaging warmth, and her brilliant coloratura voice (with a range of two and a half octaves) have made her the greatest drawing card, over an extended period, in present-day opera. Her appearance on an operatic stage usually brings long queues to the box-office, so much so that the Metropolitan Opera has revived numerous operas (such as *The Daughter of the Regiment, Tales of Hoffmann, Linda di Chamounix, Mignon, La Sonnambula*) expressly to feature her and exhibit her dazzling voice. Some years ago, more

than a half million music-lovers attended six of her concerts; at Grant Park, in Chicago, she drew 300,000 at a
single performance! In Rio de Janeiro, the police had to
be called to keep her enthusiastic public in check.

She has gathered rich honors: France made her a Chev-
alier, then an Officer, of the Legion of Honor and awarded
her the gold medal of the City of Paris; General Charles
de Gaulle presented her with the Order of the Cross of
Lorraine; in Belgium she had conferred on her the Order
of the Crown and a gold medal; she is an honorary consul
from the City of Cannes; she was adopted official daughter
of General LeClerc's Armored Division; two American
locomotives were named after her, as well as a town in
Maryland (Lilypons).

Numerous culinary dishes bear her name—a tribute,
no doubt, to her reputation as a gourmet: at the Raleigh
Hotel in Washington, D.C. they serve a "Sole Lily Pons,";
at the Madison Hotel in New York City, you can get a
"Coupe Lily Pons"; at the Carter Hotel in Cleveland, a
specialty of the house is "Chicken Lily Pons."

She has been honored for her remarkable contributions
to the war effort in World War II. With her husband,
André Kostelanetz, she traveled 100,000 miles in virtually
every theater of operation from the blazing heat of the
Persian Gulf (where, between songs, she swathed her head
with wet towels) to the numbing frost of the Belgian
front. G.I.'s in Iran, Egypt, Italy, Indo-China, Burma,
Belgium, Germany, France, etc. still recall with delight the
brief interlude of magic Lily Pons injected into their bleak
lives with her songs. The Commanding Officer of the
Indo-Burma theater awarded her with the Asiatic-Pacific
Campaign Service Ribbon, an honor only thirteen civilians
have ever received. And the United States government
gave her two citations for meritorious service.

Like Kirsten Flagstad, Lily Pons is an American discovery. Before her sensational début at the Metropolitan Opera House, Pons had sung only in small provincial theaters in France. Not until she became an idol of the American public did the rest of the world, and France with it, join in the adulation.

She was born in Cannes, on the French Riviera, on April 12, 1904. In 1907 her father, an automobile engineer, achieved momentary fame throughout Europe by embarking on the then amazing stunt of driving a Sizaire-Nandin car from Paris to Peking. He lost his way in the Urals, starved for a while in Tibet, and during the last lap of his journey was towed toward his destination.

Lily was a musical child, born with absolute pitch. In her thirteenth year she entered the Paris Conservatory, not as a singer, but as a pianist. She was an excellent pupil, won some prizes, and seemed destined for a career as piano virtuoso. A serious illness, however, frustrated these plans: her doctor forbade her to touch a keyboard for two years. When this ban was lifted, she toured Parisian hospitals playing for wounded soldiers. From time to time, she was asked to sing. To her amazement, her singing was even better received than her playing—the earliest hint that she had a good voice.

Her first professional experience as a singer took place in small rôles in the Théâtre des Variétés in Paris. A career as singer, not to mention grand opera, was still remote from her mind. In 1923, she married a retired lawyer and publisher, Mynheer August Mesritz. This marriage changed her destiny. Her husband was convinced that his wife was a singer—possibly a great singer. He engaged Signor Alberti de Gorostiaga (now known in Hollywood as Señor Alberti) to teach her. There followed a rigorous year-round regimen in which husband, wife, and teacher were virtually

inseparable. Every day in the year, for three years, Lily
worked with Signor Alberti. Fortunately, Lily had the
temperament for hard work; she had a seemingly inexhaustible vitality; she had a burning ambition to succeed. These, and more. She was a born musican, who
seemed to know instinctively the right thing to do. She
had the most extraordinary set of vocal cords of any singer
since Caruso. She had, once she began study, a voice that
was as flexible in its range as it was rich in texture; a trill
that was birdlike; an upper register that glittered like
shining silver. Signor Alberti compared her to Patti. He
said that any teacher could make a great diva out of such
material. And the Signor knew what he was speaking
about, for he was a master of *bel canto* and one of the
foremost living authorities on French vocalization.

Her début in opera did not take place until 1928. She
was introduced in Delibes' *Lakmé* (one of her great rôles)
in the Opera House at Mulhouse, Alsace. Appearances
followed in small opera houses in eighteen French cities—
valuable experience, to be sure, but not calculated to bring
her any extensive fame. In 1930—unknown in her native
land—she was given an audition at the Metropolitan Opera
House, singing the "Bell Song." Gatti-Casazza, Otto H.
Kahn, and Tullio Serafin exchanged eloquent glances, and
she was signed to a five-year contract at $445 a week. To-
day, fifteen years later, she draws from the Metropolitan
six times that figure.

Her début took place on January 3, 1931, in *Lakmé*. In
one respect, that début made history. Pons was the first
singer in more than a century to render the controversial
high note in the "Bell Song" as F instead of E-flat. Delibes
himself had changed the original E-flat to F when he discovered, to his joy, a singer who could take the higher note

Lily Pons

Ezio Pinza

easily; but not since then had any opera star attempted to duplicate the feat.

This, however, was incidental to the salient fact that Pons' voice—fresh, vital, electrifying, brilliant, projected with the utmost ease and yet in full command of every resource of vocal technique—brought back memories of the period when the art of coloratura singing was in its heyday. That period is gone, but the art itself is still kept alive, kept vibrant by the magic of the incomparable Lily.

5

EZIO PINZA

◇◇◇

W HEN EZIO PINZA made his American début
in 1926, one critic astutely referred to him as a "young
Chaliapin." The remark was prophetic. Today, with Chaliapin dead, no one seems more likely to succeed him than
Pinza. The Metropolitan Opera Association realized this
fully, for—when it planned a revival of Mussorgsky's *Boris
Godunov* for its 1938–1939 season—it selected Pinza for
the title role so long immortalized by the Russian bass.

The more one studies Pinza's performances, the more
forcefully one becomes conscious that he is Chaliapin's inevitable successor. Like Chaliapin, Pinza is much more
than a great singer. He has a magnificent voice, of course
—extraordinary for texture, range, volume, flexibility. But
with Pinza, as with his predecessor, the voice is only one
of several important elements of his art. Pinza is also a
great dramatic actor who vibrantly re-creates each rôle he
performs. It used to be said of Chaliapin—and, I believe,
by no one less than Stanislavsky of the Moscow Art Theater—that had he never chosen opera, he would have been
one of the world's great actors. This might also be said
of Pinza. Each of Pinza's operatic characterizations is as
meticulously drawn as Hamlet is in the hands of John
Gielgud or Maurice Evans.

48

When Pinza studies a new rôle, the dramatic preparation is often more intensive than the musical. He buries himself in history to understand the setting and period in which his character moves. If the character is a historical one, he absorbs all existing biographies for a more intimate understanding of the person he is trying to re-create. He will go to the museum and pore over paintings of the period for a study of costumes, and even of facial expressions; for his Don Giovanni, for example, he made a thorough study of Velásquez. Then, when the character is vivid in his mind, he will experiment with gestures and facial expressions to intensify the dramatic situations in which his character becomes involved.

Watching Pinza on the stage as Don Giovanni, Frère Laurent, Lothario, King Dodon, Oroveso, or Figaro is as much an experience for the eye as for the ear. He is a dominating figure on the stage, as compelling and magnetic as Chaliapin used to be in his tremendous impersonation of Boris. Every phase of the histrionic art has been mastered by Pinza and has become servant to the character he is trying to project. His make-up, of which he has made a science and an art; his gestures (has it ever been noticed what eloquent use he makes of his hands to accentuate a dramatic moment?); the carefully thought-out analysis of character that makes each of his rôles an integrated conception—these are qualities in Pinza's art no less striking than the authenticity, musicianship, and charm of his singing.

In one respect he has gone even beyond Chaliapin—in his amazing versatility. He has sung almost every major bass rôle in operatic literature and, being a thorough artist, has sung them all remarkably well. Italian opera is, of course, his *forte*. But he has adapted himself with incredible plasticity to the varying styles of French, German, and

Russian operas as well. His repertoire today includes more than fifty operas in almost every style of operatic writing. Who else on the operatic stage can boast of having sung so successfully in such varied operas as *Die Meistersinger, Tristan und Isolde, Mignon, Faust, Lakmé, Don Giovanni, The Marriage of Figaro, Aïda, La Juive, The Barber of Seville, Norma, Le Coq d'Or,* and *Boris Godunov?*

To his consummate art, Pinza brings personal glamour and charm, magnetism and a profile that make him footlight magic. These, even more than his magnificent voice, won Broadway completely early in 1949 when Pinza made his sensational theater début in the musical, *South Pacific,* and forthwith became the theatre's new matinee idol. They were also forcefully evident in that brief scene in *Carnegie Hall* which marked Pinza's first appearance on the screen.

Ezio Pinza was born in Rome on May 18, 1892, the youngest son of seven children. His father was a lumber dealer.

Pinza had been born so puny that he was not expected to live. Two days passed after his birth without even a christening name having been selected for him. At the end of the second day, it appeared that he might survive. It was then that a friend of the family suggested (perhaps in jest) that he be called Ezio, a pagan name forbidden by the Church. The name was accepted by the father.

A musical career for Ezio was remotest from his father's mind, who hoped to make his son a civil engineer. In Ravenna, whither the Pinza family transferred its home when Ezio was two years old, the boy began his studies preparatory to a training in engineering. But engineering was distasteful to Ezio. When he was seventeen, he abandoned his studies to become—of all things!—a professional bicycle racer. He entered in cross-country competitions and in six-day bicycle races—but only once won a prize, the second.

He tells us today that, at one time, immediately after a race, he was in a shower when suddenly he burst into song. Up to that time he had had no musical education; his only experience as a singer had been in an amateur choral club. One of his friends heard him, and laughingly told him he was a much better singer than bicycle racer, then more soberly asked him why he did not pursue the study of music. This was the first time that Pinza thought seriously of music.

He liked to sing, and he liked music; and his failure as a professional bicycle racer made him further receptive to the idea. He decided to turn to a new career. When he was eighteen he began the study of singing under Maestro Ruzza. Then, upon the death of Ruzza, Pinza became a pupil at the Conservatory of Bologna under Maestro Vezzani. He learned quickly and was soon ready for an operatic début. But the war interrupted his career. "For four years," Pinza today says, "I kept my voice on ice. I mean this not only metaphorically but literally as well—for I was a member of the Italian artillery, fighting eight thousand feet above sea level in the Alps."

When the war ended, Pinza returned to singing and made his début in the Teatro Reale dell'Opera in Rome. His rôle was that of King Mark in *Tristan und Isolde*.

He remained at the Teatro Reale for two years, growing rapidly as an artist. Then, after a short and successful engagement in Turin, he came to La Scala in Milan, to sing for three years under Toscanini. It was here that he acquired his great fame. His versatility and profound musicianship and inimitable operatic style aroused the admiration of all discriminating musicians. Toscanini himself considered Pinza one of his most capable performers. When, in 1924, Toscanini decided to give the world première of *Nerone,* by Boïto, who had died a few years earlier (an event which drew to Milan music lovers from all parts of Europe), he chose Pinza for a principal rôle.

It was at La Scala that Gatti-Casazza heard Pinza sing and engaged him for the Metropolitan Opera House.

Pinza's début at the Metropolitan took place in 1926 in Spontini's *La Vestale.* His recognition was immediate. One critic, already cited, spoke of him as a "young Chaliapin." Olin Downes reported that he was "a majestic figure on the stage; a bass of superb sonority and impressiveness."

There followed engagements in San Francisco and Chicago, then in London, Paris, and South America, and finally in Vienna and Salzburg. His popularity now became worldwide, and few there were who would not concede him a position of major importance among the opera stars of the day. In the Salzburg festivals, for a few years, he sang in *The Marriage of Figaro* and *Don Giovanni,* and was generally considered one of the major personalities of the festival and one of the great living basses.

Pinza is one of the handsomest singers in the Metropolitan Opera House—athletically built (over six feet tall, and weighing almost two hundred pounds), with dark eyes, his dark hair now slightly touched by gray. His face is finely chiseled and Romanesque; the aquiline nose descends from almond-shaped eyes toward lips that are thin and firm. The eyes have characteristic Italian intensity. He dresses smartly and shows a preference for vivid colors and checked jackets. Toward the end of 1944, a nationwide poll conducted by *Harper's Bazaar* voted Pinza one of the world's fourteen most glamorous men.

He lives on a farm in Rye, New York, with his wife (formerly a ballet dancer at the Metropolitan Opera, whom

he married in 1938), and his two children, Clelia and
Pietro. Claudia Pinza, his daughter from an earlier marriage, is today an opera singer, a member of the Metropolitan Opera company; she had made her début at a
major opera house on September 21, 1947 when she appeared with her father in a performance of Gounod's
Faust by the San Francisco Opera Company.

Pinza, in the informality of his home, has a contagious
joviality; he frequently indulges in practical jokes. At the
slightest encouragement he grows expansive about himself,
his many diversions and pastimes. Sports are probably his
major interest outside of music. He goes frequently to
boxing matches, and occasionally at home even indulges
in a round or two himself. He likes photography. He enjoys skiing, riding a bicycle, boating and fishing, and
most of all he delights in driving an automobile at breakneck speed. For indoor pastimes, he likes the movies and
funny shows (but almost never goes to the opera). He
smokes incessantly, though only half a cigarette at a time
—and that through a holder stuffed with cotton. He is an
inveterate collector: principally Roman poison rings (of
which he now has a formidable collection), pipes, watches.

He will confess, somewhat diffidently, that there is in
him a strong and uncontrollable vein of superstition. To
this day, he has retained the small and dingy dressing
room at the Metropolitan Opera House which was assigned
to him for his first appearance; he thinks it would break
his luck to change. He believes that Friday and the number 13 are lucky for him. And he clings tenaciously to a
luck-charm—a small, battered doll, which is his mascot
everywhere and which always decorates his dressing-table.
That doll was given to him many years ago by a young
girl friend, but anything beyond this—any hint of its history or of the source of its unique powers—Pinza stub-
bornly refuses to disclose.

6

LOTTE LEHMANN

◇◇◇

A RECEPTION in a New York dressing room. . . .

Rosa Ponselle, famous American singer of the Metropolitan Opera House, is being introduced for the first time
to Lotte Lehmann. Impetuously, she throws her arms
about Lehmann, kisses her ardently on both cheeks. "For-
give me," she explains simply. "I heard you sing today and
I cannot forget how deeply you moved me."

The scene shifts—to the railroad station of a Midwestern
city. Lotte Lehmann, having just finished a song recital,
is waiting with her accompanist for a midnight train. Only
one other person is on the deserted platform—a little man,
shivering with the cold. The loneliness of the night, the
long wait, and possibly the intensity of his emotions, tempt
him to essay conversation with the strangers near him.
"Did you, too, hear Lotte Lehmann's recital tonight?" he
asks. Before either of the strangers can answer, he con-
tinues, his voice quivering "She is the greatest singer on
God's earth. I have traveled a hundred miles to hear her.
A thousand miles would not have been too great for such
a privilege."

Such tributes to the singer's art epitomize, to a large extent, what the world of music—from the professional mu-

Lotte Lehmann

sician to the man-in-the-street who, untaught, loves his music instinctively—thinks of Lotte Lehmann.

Though Lehmann may not possess the technical equipment to dazzle and magnetize an audience, the appeal of her art is catholic. Not through gaudy pyrotechnics does she capture the adoration of her immense public. As a matter of fact, there are singers far less famous than she, whose range and volume are far greater than hers, and who can probably attack a bravura passage with greater sparkle and brilliance. Lehmann has a low register of dark and sensuous beauty, and a *mezza-voce* of enormous effectiveness, but to call hers a great voice, from a technical point of view, would be inaccurate.

Yet their number is legion who consider her singing one of the great aesthetic experiences that the present-day concert and opera stage has to offer. For Lehmann, whether she sings a Lied of Schubert or Hugo Wolf, or—though much less frequently now—etches a characterization of monumental stature such as her Leonore or the Marschallin, brings to the listener an unforgettable emotional experience.

Discerning intellect and impeccable taste guide every line of music she sings; often a single phrase is endowed with shattering emotional implications through the most subtle use of shading or nuance. The quality of quiet but heartbreaking pathos with which she endows the closing line of Schubert's *Gretchen am Spinnrade,* the flood of sunlight which she pours into the enchanting phrase *Sonnenschein, O Sonnenschein* by Schumann, the crushing tragedy of her portrait of a beautiful woman grown old in the first act of the *Rosenkavalier* of Richard Strauss—these are only a few of the many great moments that she achieves with passages which, at the hands of other singers, often become merely perfunctory.

She has conquered two distinct worlds of music, that of the opera and that of the concert stage, each of which requires special aptitude and talent. On the opera stage— not only in the German operas of Beethoven, Wagner, and Richard Strauss, but also in the more popular French and Italian repertory—she is an imperial figure. The best of her characterizations are etched in large and heroic lines. But her art is by no means cut to one pattern. One recalls, for example, her performance of the rôle of Christine in Strauss' *Intermezzo,* in which she executed a comic part with incomparable nimbleness and grace.

She literally dominates the stage with the magnetism of her personality. And her voice acquires amplitude, breadth, and fullness, together with her acting. On the concert stage—in her inimitable recitals of dramatic songs or Lieder—her style becomes intimate and personalized. She penetrates to the very essence of the poetic message of each song she sings; a song, with Lehmann, becomes a miniature drama. Yet such is the peculiar quality of her art in her Lieder recitals that the listener often gets the impression of a personal contact with the singer, almost as if Lehmann were singing to him and only to him.

Taste, intellect, and discernment have frequently been mentioned as qualities of Lehmann's art. Equally important is the fact that whatever she sings becomes permeated with the warm flush of her personality; and it is this quality, more than any other, that has made an entire music world her admiring public.

Her charm and geniality exert a spell in the opera house and concert hall. In Vienna she has been called the *"geliebte Lehmann"*—"beloved Lehmann." And in other music centers of the world she is esteemed no less affectionately.

Like Kreisler's violin playing, Lehmann's art is Viennese in its charm, grace, zest and warmth of heart.

She is essentially a daughter of Vienna, even though her birthplace was Germany. Her appearance is characteristically Viennese. Her figure, her round face, her intelligently expressive eyes, even her manner of wearing her hair (parted in the middle, and full around the ears), all give her appearance Viennese authenticity.

She has cultivated the Viennese art of living well and fully to a high degree. There is nothing effete or jaded about her. Her enthusiasms are many, and always fresh and alive. Her life is crowded with activity and diversion. Music, of course, is the major sphere of her activity. But Lehmann would not be a true Viennese in temperament if music, and music alone, dominated her life. She loves to read good literature—and reads it voraciously. Better still, she loves to write it. Writing to her is no mere hobby, but an essential artistic expression. At times, she finds the urge to put pen to paper almost as strong as that to sing. Creative writing, in her life, holds a place only second to that of music. She has published many poems and articles in leading magazines, and a charming novel entitled *Eternal Flight*. Her autobiography, *Midway in My Song*, and the personal history of her most celebrated opera rôles, *My Many Lives*, are suffused with the magnetism and warmth of her personality. Other books are always in the process of composition.

But Lehmann's life is so well organized that she has time not only for two exacting arts, but for lighter diversions as well—such as horseback riding and swimming, both of which she does with professional expertness. Nor did her many activities prevent her from partaking in the homely simplicity of a quiet evening with her husband, while he was alive, which afforded one of her greatest personal delights.

Her essential simplicity of character is the simplicity which has made the Viennese the most lovable people in the world. She makes no attempt to envelop herself in a self-assured glamour; postures or affectations are altogether alien to her nature. Viennese, too, is her hospitality, known to everyone who has had contact with her. In the presence of her guests, Lehmann radiates an atmosphere of conviviality and warmth of feeling which makes them feel always comfortable and at ease. Viennese is her genius for endowing any place in which she lives (even a hotel room) with the unique charm of her personality. Unfortunately, her extensive travels make it impossible for Lehmann—essentially a domestic soul—to enjoy much home life. She has several residences, her permanent one is in California. However, Lehmann has an extraordinary capacity for permeating even a transitory residence with character. There is an all-embracing cordiality in the Lehmann living room, an atmosphere of comfort and repose. No sooner does she unpack in a new setting—and every few days there is a new setting for Lehmann!—and hang her favorite portraits on the walls ("Home," she will tell you, "is where I hang my pictures"), then suddenly, as if by magic, the place acquires something of the personality of a permanent abode.

Too many writers, in describing Lehmann's personal life, have overdrawn their characterizations almost to a point of caricature. Lehmann is *not*, as some writers have suggested, a typical Viennese *Hausfrau;* she has neither the temperament nor the interest to concern herself with the management of a home. She is utterly incapable of Viennese parsimoniousness, a trait which some writers have unjustly attributed to her. Indeed, one of her great passions is the giving of extravagant presents to friends. She never comes to a city without being amply supplied with tokens for each and every one of her circle. She has a weakness for buying expensive and utterly useless knick-knacks.

A small town near Hamburg, Germany—Perleberg, not far from the North Sea—was the birthplace of Lotte Lehmann. Her childhood was not unusual. Memories of her early years today bring charming images to her mind: red plush furniture in a warm and comfortable house; her mother, all softness and solicitude; and her father, a small-town official, practical and strong-minded, who combined a love for his daughter with an insistence on strong discipline.

Herr Lehmann—at peace with the world because, being a government official, he would have a government pension when ready to retire—was determined, almost from Lotte's birth, that she should know a like blessing; and he was considering a career as schoolteacher for his daughter. From Lotte's early childhood, his energy and industry were directed toward preparing her for this field. He gave her the advantage of a well-rounded education—music, languages, drawing, the elements of science. When, many years later, Lotte Lehmann became an opera singer, Herr Lehmann's lament was that the glory of an artist, sweet though it was, was only ephemeral; only a government pension brought stability. Not until Lotte Lehmann became a permanent member of the Vienna Opera did her father know peace of mind—for, as a member of the Vienna State Opera, she was entitled to a government pension.

When Lotte was in her early teens, her family moved

to Berlin, where the plan to make her a schoolteacher continued. Enrolled in a local high school, she proved to be a bright but unenthusiastic student, more interested in the writing of poetry than in the sciences; one poem she actually sold to an editor for two dollars. And she indulged in schoolgirl flirtations and puppy-love more assiduously than in her school exercises.

As a girl, Lotte had a small and pleasant voice, with which she often entertained her close friends in performances of songs. It was through the influence of a neighbor that she was admitted to the Royal Academy of Music in Berlin. Music now absorbed her interest and awoke her enthusiasm as nothing had succeeded in doing until now, not even the writing of poetry. She was inflamed by a personal ambition for the first time in her life: she would be a concert artist.

While still a music student, Lotte Lehmann had her first serious love affair. He was a handsome, broad-chested, blond-haired young man named Willy. There were the usual whispered words, the holding of hands, the exchange of promises. Soon there was even talk of marriage, and elaborate plans for the future. Then the question of Lotte's singing arose. Willy was determined that Lotte should surrender every thought of a career and devote herself entirely to home, husband, and children. In his forceful Teutonic manner, Willy placed the decision squarely in Lotte's hands: she was to choose between a singing career and marriage. Lotte did not hesitate in her decision.

In looking back upon her first years as a music student Lotte Lehmann today recognizes what a profound debt she owes to her older brother, Fritz, now teacher of a dramatic class. His meager purse, his mature counsel, his encouragement were always at hand when Lotte needed them—and during those early years she needed all three desperately.

That her way was made so much smoother was largely the result of his conscientious devotion; and she has never forgotten this devotion.

Following her studies at the Royal Academy of Music, Lotte Lehmann became a private pupil of Mathilde Mallinger, a well-known Wagnerian singer. To Mallinger belongs the distinction of being the first to recognize Lehmann's great talent, and to guess that, with proper preparation, a magnificent career awaited her. She gave her protégée an intensive training.

Equipped with this training, which had transformed Lehmann from a blundering student into an integrated musician, she applied for a small position as singer at the Hamburg Opera House. She was given a three-year contract at a salary of two hundred marks a month (fifty dollars). Shortly after joining the opera house, she made her début as Freia in Wagner's *Rheingold*.

Her début passed without favorable notice. Some critics were even acidulously disparaging. "A Fräulein Lehmann sang and played the part of Freia with touching awkwardness," commented the *Hamburger Fremdenblatt*. "As to the vocal qualities of the young lady, whose throat seemed constricted by excessive nervousness, we can as yet say nothing." But Lehmann was not discouraged. For a long time, she continued to perform small parts.

But—though it seemed that no one was aware of her existence—her work did not pass entirely unnoticed. The musical director of the Hamburg Opera was the young but already well-known conductor, Otto Klemperer. Klemperer had silently watched Lehmann's work and had been impressed by it. Then, when the sudden illness of the Wagnerian soprano, Fleischer-Edel, demanded an immediate substitute, he approached Lehmann and asked her if she would care to try the rôle of Elsa in *Lohengrin*.

I shall let Lehmann herself describe an event which was unquestionably the turning point in her career.

"Would I care to try the rôle of Elsa? Did Herr Klemperer have to ask me *that?* I had already studied the part by myself, and I felt I knew every note of it. I came to the first rehearsal, therefore, somewhat sure of myself and my ground, and as proud as a peacock. But if I deluded myself into believing that I knew the rôle thoroughly, I was soon to see my error. Klemperer sat at the piano like some wild demon, throwing his long hands, like tiger's paws, upon the keys, guiding me by the sheer force of his fanatic will. For the first time in my life, I felt all constraining shyness fall from me completely. The rôle suddenly became the flame of my personal experience. I felt I was transfigured. I should have liked to sing this way forever, without interruption. But suddenly, a crash awakened me from my dreams. The voice of Klemperer rudely tore me from my raptures. 'You have no idea of the part,' he growled. 'You must try again, and then again, and work much more carefully.' With each lapse of memory, he would become increasingly angry and call to me, 'What is the matter *now?* I suppose Elsa's crown has turned your head!' But I was always blessed with stubbornness, and I continued working on the rôle with indefatigable ardor.

"The evening of the performance I did not see the audience; I did not even see the face of the director. I forgot everything—where I was, what the evening meant to me. I was Elsa, the Elsa that was first revealed to me by Klemperer, the Elsa that I now fully understood for the first time. Tears came to my eyes as the chorus sang *'Heil dir, Elsa von Brabant.'* And *'Heil dir'* my whole heart sings to the day of days which was the real beginning of my life."

Having been discovered by Klemperer and assigned major rôles not only in German but also in French and

Italian operas, Lehmann soon became one of the principal sopranos of the Hamburg Opera. Greater experience
brought her the self-assurance she needed. To each of her
rôles she now brought the illumination of her personality
—having acquired the self-confidence to give it full revelation—and an increasing richness of voice. The audiences
began to talk of her performances with enthusiasm.

One evening she was singing the rôle of Micaela in
Carmen. In the audience was the director of the Vienna
Court Opera who had come to Hamburg to engage its
leading tenor for several guest performances in his own
opera house. After the performance of *Carmen,* he rushed
backstage. Completely forgetting the tenor he had come
to engage, he insisted he must procure Lehmann for
Vienna.

Thus it was that Lehmann was brought to the city
where she achieved her first great triumphs, the city
which was to become her home for so many years, the
city which had known and adored another Lehmann—
the great Lilli, not related to Lotte—and which was soon
to transfer that adoration to the younger woman. In Vienna were unfolded the operatic characterizations which
were to spread Lehmann's reputation to the four corners
of the world—Sieglinde in *Die Walküre,* the Marschallin
in the *Rosenkavalier,* Leonore in *Fidelio.* In Vienna she
first emerged as a singer of dramatic songs in a series of
recitals which soon proved to be the great artistic event
of the year. It was at a rehearsal in Vienna that Richard
Strauss first heard her sing, and was so moved by her performance that he immediately designated her for the rôle
of the Young Composer in his opera *Ariadne auf Naxos.*
A few years later the master was to compose his opera
Arabella expressly for Lotte Lehmann.

As a mark of its appreciation for the great artist in its

midst, Vienna awarded Lehmann the highest decoration which the government could bestow on an artist, and with it the title of *Kammersängerin* and honorary member.

A few years later, still another government was to recognize Lehmann's genius officially—France. It appointed her an Officer of the Legion of Honor, the only woman artist of a foreign country ever to receive that award.

It was in Vienna, too, that Lotte Lehmann met Otto Krause, a dashing cavalier—formerly an officer in the Austrian army, and an extraordinary horseback rider—who might very easily have stepped from the pages of a Schnitzler novel. When Krause heard Lehmann sing at the Opera one evening, he felt as if a spell had come over him. From that time on, he was always in the opera house on the evenings that Lehmann appeared, occupying the same seat.

They met at a party. That was the beginning of a romance which was climaxed with their marriage in 1926. His death in January, 1939, was a great blow to Lehmann.

Engagements in the leading opera houses in Europe followed her triumphant successes in Vienna. Wherever Lehmann performed she was royally received. Perhaps her greatest personal victory came in Paris in 1927. For the first time since World War I, a German opera was to be introduced at the Paris Opéra—Beethoven's *Fidelio,* in honor of the centenary celebration of the composer's death. Lotte Lehmann was invited to sing the rôle of Leonore. *Fidelio* had been included in the repertory with no little misgiving. The French were still anti-German, and there was no telling how they would react to their first German opera since 1914. It was Lehmann's art, even more than Beethoven's, that conquered prejudice and hatred. An audience that greeted the opening passages of the opera with apathy was swept to enthusiasm by Lehmann's singing, until it rose to cheer her at the end of the opera. One lady is reported to have said to her neighbor: "I know I should hate her, for she is German. But how can one possibly hate a person with such a heavenly voice?"

Following successful performances at the Salzburg Festival, of which she was to become one of the major attractions for the next few years, Lehmann came to America and made her début with the Chicago Opera Company on October 28, 1930. These successful appearances in Chicago were merely the forerunners of performances throughout the country—both in opera and in recitals of Lieder—in which her prestige mounted. Finally, on January 11, 1934, she made her Metropolitan Opera House début as Sieglinde in *Die Walküre.*

"Never before," reported one critic, "in the history of the Metropolitan Opera House has there been such a success. Wagnerian audiences do not enthuse to a very great extent, but the instant the curtain fell, the applause rang out spontaneously. Then, when Lotte Lehmann came before the footlights, it rose in volume, and as her confrères left her alone—something rare in the first curtain call—the whole audience broke into cheering which lasted a full ten minutes."

Lotte Lehmann's career in America, as one of its best-loved singers of opera and song, was now fully launched.

Early in 1938, Lehmann renounced her homeland and announced that she would become a citizen of the United States. What pain this permanent separation from her beloved Vienna has brought her, only her most intimate friends know. As she herself has written in the preface of her engaging autobiography: "My blood is German and my whole being is rooted in the German soil. But my conception of art is different from that of my country. . . . I no longer understand the land of my birth."

And, just as in 1933 Lehmann renounced her native Germany, so in 1938 she broke her still stronger ties with her adopted homeland, Austria. She is now an American; the United States is her new homeland.

7

MARJORIE LAWRENCE

◇◇

In The Summer of 1941, Marjorie Lawrence, one of the world's distinguished opera singers, was in Mexico City rehearsing the rôle of Brünnhilde in *Die Walküre*. In the concluding scene, Brünnhilde reposes on a couch beneath the trees as a circle of flame arises to surround and protect her. The "Magic Fire Music" flickered and ebbed. The rehearsal ended.

Marjorie Lawrence made an effort to get off her couch, and found that she could not move a muscle.

At the American Hospital, the doctors made a terrifying diagnosis. Without any warning, she had been stricken by one of the worst cases of infantile paralysis encountered in Mexico City. It was doubtful if she would survive. It was certain that if, miraculously, she *did* live, she would be hopelessly paralyzed for life.

Tragedy, therefore, struck at her with a shattering force. She was at the height of her career, acknowledged throughout the world of music as one of the foremost living Wagnerian sopranos. Her personal life was also at a climactic point, for she had just been married to Dr. Thomas King, and was actually on her honeymoon at the time of the disaster.

One and a half years later, Marjorie Lawrence, seated

in a wheelchair, gave a song recital in Town Hall, New
York. A few months after that, still a prisoner to that chair,
she returned to the stage of the Metropolitan Opera House
to sing the role of Venus in *Tannhäuser,* a part that could
be rendered throughout in a reclining position. A year
later, she went through—and wonderfully!—one of the
most arduous roles in all opera, that of Isolde; all the
while she was strapped to a carefully camouflaged wheelchair. One year more and she was able to travel to Australia (still in a chair) covering 50,000 miles in army trans-
port planes and on jeeps, singing for more than 75,000
soldiers of the four Allied nations.

And in Chicago, on December 11, 1947, she *stood*
through an entire opera performance, in the title rôle of
Elektra. This was the first time in almost seven years that
her legs supported her in a public appearance.

Today, Lawrence fills a full-time schedule of concert
and operatic performance not only in this country but
also in Europe. Complete recovery is still a matter for the
future. But now it is merely a question of time and patience. Her victory over her infirmity, however, is complete; and surely it represents as stirring a saga of courage
as any woman has experienced in our time.

Up to the time of her tragedy, fate had been kind to her.
Success came to her comparatively quickly and decisively;
her career is not marked by a struggle for recognition.
She was born in or about 1908 in the town of Deans
Marsh, in Australia, which numbered 140 citizens, most
of whom were sheep farmers. She was five years old when
her townsfolk noticed that she had an exceptional voice.
They nicknamed her "little Melba," and not many months
passed before she was singing for them publicly in the
school auditorium or in church. The local pastor gave her
her first music lessons—voice and the piano. These had to

suffice until she was old enough to go to Melbourne. There she worked as a seamstress and a housekeeper to pay for more advanced voice lessons. In two years' time she was good enough to win first prize in an opera competition sponsored by the Melbourne *Sun*.

John Brownlee, the famous Australian singer, heard her, and convinced her that she had exceptional talent. He insisted that she go to Paris for further training. For three years, Lawrence worked in Paris with Cécile Gilly. Then, in 1932, she made her operatic debut—at Monte Carlo in *Tannhäuser*. The local critics considered her début a triumph; in fact they said that it was the most notable event in their memory since the débuts of Caruso and Chaliapin. A contract for the Paris Opéra was immediately signed. As Ortrud in *Lohengrin,* she took Paris by storm.

Edward Johnson, on a visit to Europe, heard her at the Paris Opéra and at once engaged her for the Metropolitan. Her début there on December 18, 1935 in *Die Walküre* was another jewel in the tiara of her great successes. Lawrence Gilman wrote "It should be said without further ado that this newest singer of Wagner's greater heroines is discerning and vital and alert. She has temperament and brains. She has a beautiful profile. She has an admirable sense of costume, a feeling for the stage, for the meaning of words and notes."

During the next six years, her Wagnerian characterizations gained in perspective and depth, and her singing acquired increasing richness and flexibility. There could be little doubt that she was among the great Wagnerian sopranos of the day, a fact which not even the rapidly swelling success of Kirsten Flagstad could negate.

And then the tragedy struck, and it seemed that a magnificent career had prematurely come to its end.

The anguish of the months following the tragedy need not be gone into detail here. It was sometimes a mere flip of the coin if she would live at all. But the day-by-day struggle with life was only half the tragedy. More terrible by far was the prognostication relayed one morning to her husband by her doctors: If she lived she would be paralyzed for life; her voice would be gone; her artistic career had ended.

Somehow, somewhere—possibly the reward of an active outdoor life of horseback riding, swimming, tennis, golf—she found a reserve of physical strength to fight an inevitable fate. Slowly she won her battle with death. She now steeled herself for an even greater and fiercer struggle, and with all the odds against her. She *would* sing again, and she would sing again in public. She *would* once again be the great star of opera and concert. Her husband humored her by feigning belief that such a miracle could take place. The doctors said they would do everything in their power (limited though that was) to help her; but when they left her room they shook their heads sadly. Nobody counted on what an almost superhuman will and singleness of purpose could accomplish.

It was about four months after her attack that she bravely tested her voice for the first time since the paralysis had set in. As she put it: "I couldn't stand it any longer. I just had to know about my voice—even if what I found out was the worst. I begged for a piano, and was humored. My husband strapped me to a chair and wrapped me in blankets so I could sit up, at least halfway. I wanted to sing Isolde. And I did—just a little. But enough to know deep inside of me that my voice was not impaired."

At that moment she knew that her day as an artist was not over. If it took years to resume her career, she knew she could meet that test, even at the cost of Herculean effort and patience. First she had to invent an improvised vocal technique that would enable her to sing from a seated position. This took continual experiments, painstaking breathing exercises, indefatigable voice training. Then she had to overcome her physical infirmity as best she could, so that she might have the stamina to sing strenuous roles and undertake physically exhausting tours.

She had not prepared so painstakingly for her original début as she did for her return to the concert stage at Town Hall, New York, in the fall of 1942. The curtains parted before a crowded auditorium. Marjorie Lawrence's wheelchair appeared like a throne which she occupied with regal dignity. The accompanist struck the first chords, and the soprano raised her voice. "It is astonishing but true," reported one critic, "that her voice . . . is just as powerful and eloquent as ever and actually more brilliant in its top levels."

She had met her first test, and met it brilliantly. But would she be able to duplicate this feat in an actual opera performance, victim as she was to a wheelchair? The answer came on the evening of January 22, 1943 at the Metropolitan Opera House in Wagner's *Tannhäuser*. Before the curtains parted, the soprano was wheeled to the stage and there gently lifted and deposited on a divan, where—as the part of Venus demands—she could recline for the entire act. The audience, sensitive to the drama of the evening, awaited the ending of the "Venusberg Music" for the soprano's first notes. They came, and there was no doubt that they were as wondrous as they had ever been. When the scene was over, Lawrence was given one of the most moving ovations seen at the Metropolitan Opera House. It was an ovation inspired by a great performance; and the audience was not thinking of Venus.

Today Marjorie Lawrence is in full mastery of her art.

She is as great in the opera house and concert hall as she had been before 1941, and in some respects her art has acquired mellowness, sensitivity and maturity it did not have before. But she still has to work hard at her physical exercises in preparing for each and every appearance. She practises standing for half an hour at a time; then for an hour; and finally for longer periods. She is learning to walk as a child does, a few yards without support, longer distances with it. Her doctors now concede that the impossible has taken place: not only has she been able to return to her career, but complete recovery seems now certain. And there is nothing in their medical books that can explain how this has happened.

One of Lawrence's greatest sources of inspiration during her dark hours came from a man who had also suffered the same disease at the prime of his life but who, in spite of such a handicap, rose to become a four-time President of the United States, and a world leader in one of history's life-and-death struggles. When she gave her first recital in New York following the tragedy, she received a letter from that man; today it is one of her most treasurable possessions. It reads:

"Your courage and faith and determination in overcoming the after-effects of infantile paralysis and thereby restoring to the public the opportunity of enjoying your beautiful art—all result in a victory—your victory—which is an inspiration to everyone at any time. . . .

"Mirrored in your great victory for many years to come, those beset with the burdens and harassed with handicaps will see the glory and the satisfaction of the good fight—well won.

"From an old veteran to a young recruit, my message to you is: 'Carry on!'

"Cordially yours, Franklin D. Roosevelt."

8

LAWRENCE TIBBETT

❖◇◇

LIKE SOME COLOSSUS, Lawrence Tibbett bestrides
the world of music with one foot in the opera house and
the other in the concert hall. His operatic fame is, of
course, worldwide—a fame won by a baritone voice that
is spacious and eloquent, and by a series of operatic characterizations (Iago, the elder Grémont, Scarpia, Simon
Boccanegra, Ford, Tonio, Emperor Jones) that are unforgettable for dramatic truth and warm humanity. As one
French critic said of him, "He belongs to the race of grand
lyric tragedians."

But he is also a master on the concert stage. With a
repertory of almost five hundred songs, he has proved that
he is as notably an artist of the lyric style as of the dramatic. None of the magnetism and excitement of a Tibbett
performance is lost, even when deprived of the glamorous
trappings of an operatic set, costumes, and dramatic text.
A great voice, a vibrant personality, a penetrating interpretative insight combine in Tibbett to make a recital as
exhilarating an experience as an operatic performance.
He is today one of the best-loved figures on the American
concert stage, with more than a thousand recitals to his
credit.

One-time sailor, newsboy, cowhand, and jack-of-all-

trades, Lawrence Tibbett has found that he can today command a king's ransom for doing what he likes best to do
anyway, even if he were not paid to do so: singing. "Singing," he has confessed, "is just about the best fun the
human animal can have. It is a gorgeous sensation, simply
because a tone is the most perfect expression of emotion."
Tibbett likes to sing for the sake of singing; and he likes
to sing because he is unashamedly fond of having audiences listen to him. He often speaks of himself as "an old
trouper" at heart. It has been estimated that he travels
about 25,000 miles annually in this country to fill his
numerous engagements. He loves every mile of it—the
grind, the fatigue, the nervous strain, the perpetual change
and movement. In short, he likes his profession; and the
joy he takes in what he is doing explains, at least partly,
the wonderful gusto of his performances.

Completely unassuming and democratic, Tibbett has an
informal American hail-fellow-well-met attitude that en-
dears him to all who have any contact with him. Whether
he is in his spacious and beautifully outfitted apartment
in New York, or on his beloved seventy-two-acre farm at
Wilton, Connecticut, he reveals a wholesome simplicity
that is engaging. You won't find a retinue—butler, valets,
servants—at the Tibbett house, though his enormous income could well run to such indulgences; no suggestion
there of swank. At his farm he wears his old clothes, attends to the garden, pitches hay, helps with the preparation of the meals. In his New York home, if he is less
rustic, he is not much more formal or pretentious. He entertains his intimate friends without display of any kind,
and usually with a great deal of music-making. His diversions are not many. He has the American love of speed—
driving a car or a boat at breakneck pace. But he also indulges occasionally in fishing, walking, and mountain-

climbing. One of his ambitions is to climb Mt. Rainier and Mt. Hood.

Obviously, there is not a trace of snobbery to the man— and that goes in his music as well as in his private life. He likes good music, whether it is grand opera and oratorio, or operetta and jazz. His programs will often include the so-called more popular brand of song because Tibbett thinks that, in its own *genre,* such a song is very good and that the public wants to hear it. He puts it this way: "The 'arty' group who turn up their noses at having popular songs on a concert program are like the people who rave about antiques and think any old thing is good, if it is old enough."

It is his intense democratic spirit that compelled him, along with other famous and far-sighted musicians (including Heifetz), to organize AGMA, of which he has been the president. AGMA is a society for the protection of the rights of the less-known concert artist who, because of his unique status as a concert performer, is not eligible to join any existing labor union. The established and famous artists like Tibbett and Heifetz have nothing to gain from it. At one time, James Caesar Petrillo, president of the American Federation of Musicians, asked Tibbett how much he earned as president of AGMA. "Why," answered Tibbett, "nothing at all." Petrillo for a moment was stupefied into silence—that a man should be willing to give so much time, effort, and energy to a venture that brought him no personal gain! Suddenly Petrillo's eyes brightened. "Oh, I understand," he said wisely. "You are making a comfortable berth for yourself against the time when you won't be able to sing any longer!"

Not the least of Tibbett's appealing qualities are his love of fun and his passion for indulgence in harmless pranks on unsuspecting victims. Once he perpetrated a jest that Hollywood did not soon forget. He was a guest at a fashionable party, where he was asked to perform. He announced that he would sing a "wonderful song" by "a little-known Russian genius named Kovlikovovsky." Then, without accompaniment, he improvised a melody of his own invention, fitted to words that were sheer gibberish. "I sobbed, I laughed, I waved my hands, making up words and music as I went along." The audience was fascinated, called the song simply wonderful, and made a mental note to remember the name of "that genius Kovlikovovsky," but the cream of the jest appeared a few moments later. An exotic actress—she *said* she was of the Russian nobility—came up to Tibbett to congratulate him. A bit embarrassed at having tried to fool a prominent Russian, Tibbett apologized: "I'm sorry that my Russian accent is so terrible that none of the words can have been intelligible." "On the contrary," beamed the actress, "it was wonderful. I understood every word."

He comes of pioneer American stock, born in Bakersfield, California, on November 16, 1896. (Originally, he spelled his name Tibbet; but when he made his first Metropolitan Opera House appearance, the program printer misspelled it with a double-t—and Tibbett has retained this spelling ever since.) He has described his early background as follows: "My people came to California in the 1849 Gold Rush and settled in as pioneer farmers. My great-uncle planted the first navel-orange tree in California, from which sprang one of the great industries of the State. . . . Most of my forebears were sheriffs, or had something to do with the enforcement of law in a land that was almost lawless. My own father was sheriff of Bakersfield. He might have stepped out of a Wild West novel, for those were the days of bandits and stagecoach hold-ups, and he was constantly at war with outlaws. Later, he was shot dead by Jim McKinney, one of California's famous outlaws. I was six then, but already my father was a magnificent hero to me, and remained so for many, many years. He left me a vivid inheritance of outdoor life that gave me much romance and virility and it has fed me ever since.

"Poverty struck hard at us then, and we moved down to Los Angeles. My mother and my three older brothers and a sister all worked hard to keep things going. While I was growing up, I put in each summer on a cattle ranch, where I took part with the cowboys in their round-ups. I took to hunting early, and, when quite a boy, spent two years in the mountains. I remember shooting my first deer at ten with a gun much bigger than myself. They were glorious days, good for mind and body alike."

In his twelfth year, Tibbett entered the Manual Arts High School in Los Angeles. There he acted in the school plays and did some singing. He loved the singing particularly. The principal of the school recalls to this day a conversation he had with the boy just before his graduation. "Which will it be for you, Larry—Hollywood and the movies, or Broadway and the stage?"

"Neither," answered the boy firmly. "It will be the Metropolitan Opera House—and singing."

"Soon my turn came to earn a living," Tibbett recalls further. "Mother had taught me singing and encouraged me from an early age. I became a church soloist, and earned small but regular remuneration. Week-end work in a newspaper office swelled the earnings. Small theater parts came my way, too. Wartime found me with good work on a training ship. I traveled widely, and returned to the States with ambition keener than ever. Then came hard times. I formed and directed a male quartet, and we

used to sing at churches, weddings, and even funerals—
anything that would bring money. I had a terrific time for
several years—'nip and tuck' all the time. Then my luck
turned. I was given work singing in the musical prologues
that used to precede the movies in those days."

That movie job was at the Grauman Theater in Hollywood. Unfortunately, Tibbett did not hold on to it. At one
of the performances, he missed a cue, pandemonium ensued, and he had to hunt another job. For a while, he
worked in several light opera companies, singing in operettas by Gilbert and Sullivan and Victor Herbert. The
study of singing was also begun seriously—for the first time
in his life—first with Basil Ruysdael, then in New York
with Frank La Forge.

He had two auditions with the Metropolitan Opera
Association before he was given a contract. The salary was
$60 a week, and the rôles he was to sing were minor ones—
but it *was* a beginning. His début took place on November 24, 1923, in *Boris Godunov,* Tibbett singing the part
of the monk. It would have required more prophetic
vision than critical perspicacity to have recognized in that
début the birth of one of the most triumphant operatic
careers of our times. Actually, nobody did. Nor did subsequent performances give even a suggestion of his future
greatness.

Then, with dramatic suddenness, there took place an
event which the *New York Times* described as "without
precedent in the annals of the Metropolitan." Surely it
was one of the most memorable and one of the epically
historic evenings in the entire history of the opera-house.
The Metropolitan was reviving Verdi's *Falstaff,* and at the
zero hour the singer responsible for the part of Ford
was incapacitated. Tibbett knew the part well and volunteered to act as substitute. What happened on the evening

of January 2, 1925, is now history. The freshness and humor and vivacity which Tibbett brought to his part—together with a burst of beautiful singing, especially in the second act—inspired an ovation which was one of the most stirring personal tributes ever experienced by an artist in those hallowed halls. Tibbett's performance, which in the words of the *New York Times* was "exemplary in its sincerity and dramatic feeling, its justness of accent, and its excellent vocal quality," placed him at once in the front rank of the opera stars of the day.

This was no ephemeral triumph. It was the beginning of a magnificent career. With subsequent appearances—now in starring rôles—Tibbett grew rapidly. His self-assurance and poise developed by his success in *Falstaff,* his operatic personality became enriched. In one successful appearance after another—*The King's Henchman, Simon Boccanegra, Otello, Jonny spielt auf!, Peter Ibbetson, Emperor Jones, Pagliacci, Tosca, Peter Grimes,* surely a varied enough repertoire to test the versatility of any artist—his hold on his audiences grew more and more tenacious. The triumph that sounded for Tibbett on the evening of January 2, 1925, was to continue for many years, and, as a matter of fact, has not yet subsided.

9

MARIAN ANDERSON

THE SUCCESS of Marian Anderson represents the triumph of genius over the greatest single obstacle an artist can be called upon to hurdle: race prejudice. There have been excellent Negro musicians before Anderson, and comparatively successful ones, too. But none, not even so sensitive an artist as Roland Hayes, has risen so high as she. To call Marian Anderson the greatest living Negro musician, as so many have done, is to qualify her reputation unwarrantably. She is more than that: she is one of the great artists of our generation *regardless* of race, color, or nationality. And, in some respects, she stands alone, majestic, incomparable.

Both as artist and as human being she holds a regal position in music with rare stateliness. In her art, she has ever clung tenaciously to the highest standards alone; one can go through her career with microscopic thoroughness without discovering any hint of concession to expediency. So, in her everyday life, she has always behaved with rare integrity and dignity. I do not refer to her many benefactions to her race, which she prefers to keep unpublicized; I refer rather to the noble spirit and the beautiful pride with which, throughout her life, she has walked in spite of the prejudice, the hatred, the ignorance surrounding her. This is what was meant when the Spingarn award given her in 1939 carried the additional citation: "Equally with that achievement which has won her worldwide fame as one of the greatest singers of our time, is her magnificent dignity as a human being."

She has never descended to the level of those who have been hostile because of their color; on the contrary, she has always worn her color as a medal of honor. It is her practice to include at least one group of Negro Spirituals in every program, not because it is expected of her, but because it is the music of her race, the eloquent and poignant voice of her people. It is also her practice, when she appears on the stage of any concert hall that segregates Negroes, to bow to her own people first, and only afterwards to the rest of the audience. She does this simply, unostentatiously, almost with humility—telling the world that she cannot forget that she is a Negro, only because the world refuses to let her race forget its color.

The climax of her lifelong struggle against race prejudice came during the first months of 1939. Her manager tried to hire Constitution Hall in Washington, D. C., for a recital in February, 1939. Because the Daughters of the American Revolution looked with undisguised disfavor on the appearance of a Negro in Constitution Hall, the theater was barred to her. Such barefaced discrimination evoked a chorus of protest throughout the country. Musicians, statesmen, clergymen, writers, vehemently denounced the D.A.R., and Mrs. Franklin D. Roosevelt resigned from that organization. Secretary of the Interior Harold L. Ickes then invited Miss Anderson to give her concert at the Lincoln Memorial. She consented, offering to sing for nothing to whoever cared to come to listen. On April 9, an audience of 75,000 assembled before the

Memorial, among them Supreme Court judges, Congressmen, Cabinet members; and another audience of several millions heard the concert over the radio. She sang Lieder and Negro Spirituals. Before her stretched an enthusiastic throng which was paying homage in no uncertain terms to a great artist. Behind her loomed the massive and benign figure of Abraham Lincoln, seeming almost to serve as spiritual godfather to the proceedings. (This concert, incidentally, is the subject of a mural design decorating the new Department of the Interior Building, in Washington, D. C.)

One week later, at a concert at Carnegie Hall, a capacity audience rose to its feet spontaneously when Marian Anderson came onto the stage, and gave her one of the most impressive demonstrations ever to be seen in that august hall. Here, surely the Daughters of the American Revolution had their answer: *this,* after all, was America, and not Nazi Germany.

It is true that this occurrence put Marian Anderson's name on the front page of every newspaper in the country, threw the limelight of national publicity sharply on her. But it revealed either an abysmal ignorance of the truth, or a blinding prejudice, to say (as Westbrook Pegler did at the time) that it was this that transformed an obscure singer into a famous one. Marian Anderson obscure in 1939? Here are the facts.

In August, 1935, she electrified what is perhaps the most discriminating music audience in the world at the Mozarteum in Salzburg—an assemblage of world-famous musicians, aesthetes, journalists, critics. "A voice like yours," remarked Toscanini, who was at that concert, "comes once in a century." A half-year later, she gave that concert in Town Hall, New York, at which she was unreservedly acclaimed one of the greatest concert artists of our gener-

ation—"mistress of all she surveyed," as the critic of the
New York *Times* put it. Her concert at Carnegie Hall, a
a month later, was sold out in advance. She was invited
to sing at the White House before President and Mrs.
Roosevelt. An extensive European tour followed. In the
Soviet Union, she expected to stay one month, but such
was her success that she had to stay three. In Vienna, she
sang under Bruno Walter to triumphant acclaim. In Fin-
land, Sibelius was so stirred by her singing that he dedicated one of his songs to her, *Solitude.* Concerts in Spain,
Switzerland, Monte Carlo, Scandinavia, Egypt, Palestine,
South America (in Buenos Aires she gave twelve consecutive concerts to full houses!) were scenes of personal triumph. Again, between January 2 and May 28, 1938, she
traveled 26,000 miles and gave 70 concerts (believed to be
the most ambitious tour ever undertaken by any artist).
By this time, her concerts in New York were automatically
sold out weeks in advance, while an appearance abroad had
to be booked two years ahead. On July 2, 1939, she was
given the Spingarn medal for the greatest achievement by
a Negro "in an honorable field of endeavor."

By 1939, she had arrived at the full richness of her vocal
powers. As Toscanini suggested, her voice was truly without equal, gracefully spanning as it did three full octaves
without betraying a flaw. In sheer beauty of tonal production, in variety of colors from the deep purple of her low
tones to the bright crimson of her falsetto, her voice was
like a Stradivarius in the hands of Heifetz. Destiny had
indeed given her an incomparable instrument, and she
did justice to it. With voice were combined brains and
scholarship, heart and sensitivity, taste and refinement.
Simply, she brings a wealth of humanity and culture to
every song she sings in her extensive repertoire of more
than two hundred compositions, whether an aria by Pur-

cell, a Lied by Brahms, or a Spiritual. She fashions a lyric line as Casals used to do on the 'cello, each note having its precise rôle to fill, and assuming its inevitable place in the design of the whole. Drama and heightened tragedy she brings with the most economical use of shade and nuance: I have heard many world-famous Lieder singers interpret the chant of Death in Schubert's *Death and the Maiden*, but no one that I can recall brought such an overwhelming sense of doom as Anderson did merely through the subtle use of tints and hues. She can change her mood magically, as she draws from Scarlatti or Handel or Schubert or Brahms or Hugo Wolf the very essence of their art. A mistress of all she surveys. . . .

Her rendition of Negro Spirituals is, of course, a deeply personal expression. To these songs she brings the full tragedy of a race despised and rejected. *Nobody Knows de Trouble I've Seen*—the expression of sorrow becomes more poignant and heartbreaking because of the restraint with which she speaks her woe. *Were You There When They Crucified My Lord?*—she brings the immense and shattering sorrow of one who knows what it means to be crucified. *Deep River*—with those unequaled low tones of hers, luscious in texture, the melody acquires wings and soars as never before.

Marian Anderson was born in South Philadelphia in 1908. Her father sold coal, and his income was so meager that her mother (an ex-schoolteacher) had to supplement it by taking in washing. But Marian's was not an unhappy childhood. Music brought a glow and warmth into the Anderson household. On many an evening, the family gathered with friends to sing Spirituals.

Singing, from the first, was both an artistic compulsion

and a financial necessity for Marian. When she was six, she made her first public appearance singing in a duet at the Union Baptist Church. Soon after this, she joined its junior choir, graduating into the senior choir after seven years. At the same time, she helped support her family by singing at church concerts, earning money that was even more needed after 1920, on the death of her father. She had earned her first singing fee (fifty cents) when she was eight years old, but before many years had passed she was paid as much as $25 a performance. In a community where dollars were not plentiful, and incomes were small, this eloquently attests to her extraordinary popularity with her neighbors.

At the South Philadelphia High School her voice attracted a Negro actor named Thomas Butler, who recommended her to her first voice teacher, Mary S. Patterson. A few months later, the Philadelphia Choral Society held a benefit concert for her, the profits of which enabled her to become a pupil of Agnes Reifsnyder.

She was seventeen when the principal of South Philadelphia High School urged the well-known vocal teacher, Giuseppe Boghetti, to accept her as a pupil. Her lessons were paid for by the nickels and dimes gathered among the members of her church. To this day, Boghetti recalls the audition. It was dusk. Behind him lay a hard day of teaching. He was too weary even to put on the lights. Sinking deep into his chair, he motioned to the somewhat self-conscious visitor to sing. She sang *Deep River,* and "it was as if the sun had suddenly flooded the rooms."

She worked industriously under Boghetti, and made such rapid progress that, in a few months, her teacher made ambitious plans for her. She gave a recital at Witherspoon Hall in Philadelphia, and another at Town Hall in

New York. She also entered a contest conducted by the New York Philharmonic at the Lewisohn Stadium. There were 300 contestants. Marian—singing *O Mio Fernando*—won the prize: an appearance with that orchestra. The impression she made was so profound that she was engaged for an appearance with the Philadelphia Orchestra. A concert manager signed her to a contract.

But engagements were not easy to get. She was unknown; she was a Negro. Even some of those who themselves were not prejudiced, and who were ready to acknowledge that she sang magnificently, would not sponsor her for fear of unfavorable public reaction. "If only she was not a Negro," they would say sadly. That she was rejected, not because she was artistically inadequate, but because of her race, was a galling dose to take. But Anderson would not yield to bitterness, nor descend to hatred. She brushed aside her disappointment and worked all the harder.

Her manager decided that the climate of Europe might be healthier for a Negro singer. She went to London where many leading musicians, amazed by her singing, worked for her. Roger Quilter arranged for her to give a recital; Sir Henry J. Wood invited her to appear as soloist at the Promenade Concerts; Ernest Newman wrote an article praising her artistry.

The Julius Rosenwald Scholarship, which she won in 1929, enabled her to travel and study for a few years. Finally, an appearance in Berlin in 1933 (for which, incidentally, she had to pay $500!) launched an extensive concert tour that brought her to France, Belgium, Holland, Italy, Scandinavia, the Soviet Union. And in August, 1935, there took place the Salzburg concert with which her wonderful career as an artist of first importance can be said have begun.

It was a historic concert, and it has been eloquently described by Vincent Sheean.*

"Into the wealth of European classical and romantic music that was heard in Salzburg in 1935, there was introduced a note that was new and strange. A musical hostess, Mrs. Moulton, invited three or four hundred people to an afternoon of songs at the Hôtel de l'Europe. The guests included Toscanini, Lotte Lehmann, Bruno Walter, and practically all the other musical powers of Salzburg. The artist was Marian Anderson. I do not think anybody there had heard her before. . . . She sang Bach, Schubert, and Schumann, with a final group of Negro Spirituals. Her superb voice commanded the closest attention of that audience from its first note. The Archbishop was sitting in the front row, and at his insistence she repeated the Schubert *Ave Maria*. In the last group she sang a spiritual, *They Crucified My Lord, and He Never Said a Mumblin' Word*. Hardly anybody in the audience understood English well enough to follow what she was saying, and yet the immense sorrow—something more than the sorrow of a single person—that weighted her tones and lay over her dusky, angular face was enough. At the end of the spiritual, there was no applause at all—a silence instinctive, natural, and intense, so that you were afraid to breathe. What Anderson had done was something outside the limits of classical or romantic music: she frightened us with the conception, in musical terms, of course, but outside the normal limits, of a mighty suffering. Without the conventional training of an art-singer she would probably never have been able to do this, and yet she did it most of all by a quality of tone and expression which transcended even her rare gift and related her to millions of others; it was most of all a racial quality. To find it in a great singer was something that had not happened before. It made some of the more self-conscious of our Festival manifestations seem

* *Between the Thunder and the Sun.* Copyright, 1943, by Vincent Sheean. Reprinted by permission of Random House, Inc.

pallid and absurd. Anderson's tragic muse, coming from a world outside the formal design and limited aspiration of a baroque town, seemed too much to be contained there, and even at moments when it was most wedded to German romantic music (as in Schubert's *Aufenthalt*) invested the whole with barbaric wildness, a sheer tribal terror, for which our experience gave us no clue. She had two recitals in Salzburg, one private and one public, and we went away from both in a kind of thoughtful daze, since the problems posed (all unconsciously, no doubt) by her phenomenal singing were in fact beyond the range of art."

In December, 1945, a testimonial dinner was given to Marian Anderson honoring the tenth anniversary of her historic début in New York. The great of the music world attended to pay tribute to a fellow artist. In these ten years, she had given more than 700 concerts in 289 cities at which more than four million attended. She had been selected for five consecutive years by national polls as the foremost woman singer over the radio. She had established the Marian Anderson Award—initially with the $10,000 Bok Award she received from the city of Philadelphia in 1941, and subsequently with additional funds from her own pocket—to help the careers of young, struggling singers. (One of the recipients of this award, Camilla Williams, has already made her mark in opera and concerts.) In short, in these ten years, Marian Anderson has proved herself to be one of the great artists of our time, and one of its great women. As Fannie Hurst put it: "Marian Anderson has not grown simply great, she has grown great simply."

In July, 1943, she was married to an architect, Orpheus H. Fisher, and since that time she has made her permanent home in a 105 acre farm near Danbury, Connecticut. She is inordinately proud of her livestock and her crops, and the income she derives from her produce thrills her more than the large sums she receives from her concert work. Her principal regret is that she can spend so little time at home: Her extraordinary success necessitates extensive traveling throughout the country and for the greater part of the year. In traveling, she takes six pieces of luggage, only one of which contains her clothing; in the others will be found a portable phonograph, sewing machine, electric iron, and a variety of cooking utensils. When on the road, she prefers cooking her own meals whenever possible, and she goes in for sewing when she feels the need of relaxation.

10

JAN PEERCE

A CAREER like that of Jan Peerce could have happened nowhere but in a country like this which breeds unorthodox careers. It began in a synagogue in the slums of New York. It continued in the so-called "borscht" circuit in the Catskill Mountains. It developed in a Broadway motion-picture theatre. Throughout all of this, his musical training was haphazard to say the least. That rigorous apprenticeship that most singers must serve in minor opera houses and concert halls before challenging fame did not exist for him.

Yet he developed into America's foremost tenor of opera and concert, and one of the great Italian tenors of our day. His artistry has brought back to opera performances a bit of the luster that died with Enrico Caruso. In the concert halls of the country (Peerce's annual tours cover more than 50,000 miles a season) his beautiful singing has won him an acclaim few other singers receive.

His appeal is exclusively a musical one. On the stage, he has little of that personal magnetism and glamour that casts a spell on an audience before a single note is sounded. Awkward, even somewhat self-conscious, the first impression he makes on an audience is by no means a striking one. He is short, stubby, barrel-chested, looking more like an insurance salesman than an artist. Away from the stage, his modest and reticent existence (he lives in New Rochelle, N. Y., with his wife and three children in a seclusion he guards jealously) is incapable of inspiring the kind of publicity that makes for front-page news.

But then he raises his voice in song—and the audience is his, and he becomes vibrant news. Sure in placement, flexible in range, sensitively projected, expressive in quality, his is one of the most beautiful tenor voices of our day. A natural understanding of *bel canto*, a penetrating insight into the artistic refinements of a song or an aria, a purity of diction, and a fine sense of style indicate that a wonderful instrument has found a deserving artist. No wonder, then, that everywhere he sings he wins his audiences decisively. Arturo Toscanini has referred to him as "my favorite tenor," and has had him appear as soloist under his direction a dozen or so times. And the Maestro, whose historic association with the world's opera houses over a period of half a century has brought him into direct contact with the greatest tenors of our generation, should know whereof he speaks!

Jan Peerce was born as Jacob Pincus Perelmuth in the slums of New York's East Side where his father operated a modest catering establishment. His parents had come from Russia in that tidal wave of immigration that swept over this country in the last decades of the 19th century. Jacob was their first-born, for whose future they had ambitious plans. Specifically, they wanted him to become a doctor (they planned his schooling accordingly). They also wanted him to get a smattering of culture, and began violin lessons for him when he was nine years old.

Singing was for him as natural a process as eating or breathing. The scales and double-stops over which he labored so painstakingly on his violin was a chore he went through bravely. But when he wanted musical satisfaction it was not his violin that provided it, but his voice. He sang continually for his own pleasure—and sometimes, when the choir of the Attorney Street Synagogue could use him, for a fee. Even when he helped organize a little jazz band in which he played the violin—performing at neighborhood dances—he was found more often singing refrains than playing his instrument.

In his fifteenth year he joined the Musicians Union which enabled him to get a job in the Catskill Mountains in New York. The Catskills—which has earned the picturesque sobriquet of "borscht" circuit—was Jacob's principal scene of musical activity for the next fourteen summers. In these years he abandoned the original plan of becoming a doctor, and convinced himself that his place would be in music, popular music. He played in his jazz band and he sang the vocal refrains. As the years passed, he continued preparing himself for a career in popular music, and dreamed of the time when he would graduate out of the "borscht" circuit into "big time."

He was playing and singing at the golden anniversary dinner of Weber and Fields at the Waldorf Astoria in September of 1932—his rendition of *Yours Is My Heart Alone* received a particularly nice hand—when an engraved visiting card was brought to him. "Roxy," the celebrated movie impresario of the Radio City Music Hall, who was present at the dinner, asked Peerce to visit him at his office the following morning.

"I have two sound pieces of advice to give you," "Roxy" told him at that meeting. "One—throw away your violin and take to singing seriously. Two—change your name from Jacob Pincus Perelmuth to something that looks better in lights. If you follow both suggestions, I'm ready to give you a four-week trial contract at the Music Hall for $250 a week."

Jan Peerce (it was "Roxy" who concocted the new name), now a member of the country's leading motion-picture theatre, prepared for his début. But, at the zero hour, his song was deleted from an overlong stage show. "I spent that evening in the wings, crying like a kid," he later confessed. But even worse luck followed. "Roxy" fell ill. The new singer was forgotten in the ensuing confusion. The four-week contract appeared ready to lapse before Jan Peerce could sell himself.

He was loitering disconsolately backstage when Erno Rapee, the music director, came upon him, listened to the sad recital of his misfortune, and promised to find a spot for him. Rapee did, at the very next show: an offstage rendition of *Play, Fiddle Play!* The song stopped the show. Peerce was immediately engaged as a permanent member of the Music Hall company.

During the next five years, Peerce's singing was one of the major attractions of the Music Hall. In that period he appeared more than 2,370 times before audiences numbering more than 15,000,000. He was also heard across the country on the national hookup program broadcast each Sunday from the Music Hall. His popularity over the air was as great as in the theatre. Before long, he was appearing extensively on major radio programs sponsored by Coca-Cola, Ford, General Motors, etc. Then he acquired an important program of his own, "Great Moments in Music." And his reputation over the radio had grown through the years: In 1946, a national poll among radio critics selected him as radio's leading male singer.

Meanwhile, he was preparing himself for what he knew would eventually be his lifework: serious music. In his broadcasts on the Sunday Music Hall hour he was permitted a more ambitious repertoire. He not only sang the masterpieces in song literature, but also appeared in abridged versions of great operas. These brief excursions into the world of great music convinced him that a swollen weekly check was no substitute for the personal satisfaction that came with making great music. He now began studying the voice intensively for the first time, principally with Giuseppe Boghetti. He worked painstakingly on his vocal technique which up to now he had applied with more instinct than science, and on his repertoire. He did not know when or how he would make the transition from a motion-picture theatre and the radio to the concert hall and opera house. But he knew that when an opportunity would arise enabling him to make that change he would be ready for it.

That opportunity came sooner than he expected. In February, 1938, Samuel Chotzinoff, music director of the National Broadcasting Company, arranged for Peerce to have an audition with Arturo Toscanini. When Peerce offered to sing the aria *Una furtiva lagrima* from *L'Elisir d'Amore*, the maestro himself sat down at the piano to play the accompaniment.

"It took supreme effort and will power to compel myself to forget where I was and who was sitting there at the piano playing the accompaniment," he later told an interviewer. "I looked out of the window, watched the snow fall, and sang the best I could."

The best, obviously, was good enough. *"Che bella voce!"* ("What a beautiful voice!") Toscanini exclaimed. There and then he engaged Peerce to sing the tenor part in a projected Carnegie Hall performance of Beethoven's Ninth Symphony.

Toscanini's approval, together with the success of that

Marian Anderson

Jan Peerce

appearance under the Maestro's baton, were the passports
he needed to enter the world of serious music.

Early in 1939, Peerce began the first of his extensive
concert tours, making an impressive New York début on
November 7 of that year. In 1941, he entered the Metropolitan Opera House, making his bow in *La Traviata,* in
the rôle of Alfredo. Since then he has appeared as the
principal tenor of both the Metropolitan Opera and the
San Francisco Opera companies, as a guest artist with other
major opera companies, as a busy recitalist and guest performer with most of our great symphony orchestras, and
as a radio singer and recording artist.

The choirboy of an East Side synagogue and the ballad-
ist of a Broadway movie house was now America's foremost tenor. Like Minerva springing from the head of
Jupiter, he was born to greatness, full-grown.

11

JOHN CHARLES THOMAS

◇◇◇

J AN PEERCE graduated from a Broadway motion-picture theatre. Another beloved American singer, the baritone John Charles Thomas, came from the Broadway musical-comedy.

The town of his birth was Meyersdale, Pennsylvania; the year, 1891. The son of a Methodist minister, he frequently joined his father and mother in singing at camp meetings where his father preached. His earliest ambition was to emulate his father. Then he was attracted to medicine, and actually entered the Mount Street College of Homeopathy in Baltimore to specialize in surgery. Music was a diversion and pleasure which never palled; but it was a long time before he thought seriously of making it his life work.

While studying surgery in 1910, he won a scholarship at the Peabody Conservatory in Baltimore. He was faced with a choice: medicine or music? He did not know which to adopt. He tossed a coin and allowed Fate to make the decision for him. It dictated music.

After studying with Blanche Blackman and Adelin Fermin at the Peabody Conservatory, Thomas joined the Henry Savage Opera Company, which gave an extensive repertory of operettas. This proved a stepping-stone to

Broadway. In *The Peasant Girl* he scored a decisive hit, beginning a long and successful reign as matinee idol. He sang in *The Passing Show* of 1913, in the Gilbert and Sullivan repertory starring DeWolf Hopper (1914), and in a series of lovable operettas including Fritz Kreisler's *Apple Blossoms* and Sigmund Romberg's *Maytime*. Like Grace Moore, he could now command a fabulous salary, and, like Grace Moore, he renounced it for a greater career as an opera star and concert singer. He never wavered in his decision to aspire to heights greater than Broadway. "I stayed long enough to save enough money to enable me to begin concert work seriously," he has explained.

He made his concert début in 1918, and his initiation in opera took place six years later in Washington, D. C., in a local performance of *Aïda*. In 1925 he went to Europe, auditioned at the Théâtre de la Monnaie in Brussels, and was given a contract. His début there in *Hérodiade* was so successful that his original contract was destroyed, and a new three-year one drawn up. During this period, Thomas sang fifteen major rôles, including one in the world première of Milhaud's *Les Malheurs d'Orphée*. This apprenticeship behind him (and a valuable one it proved to be!), he sang in London, Berlin, and Vienna, and always successfully. In 1930, he returned to America, appearing first with the Chicago Civic Opera (*Pagliacci*), then in Philadelphia and San Francisco. At last, on February 2, 1934, he appeared at the Metropolitan Opera House in *La Traviata*. His singing, as one critic wrote, was marked by "opulence of volume, polish in quality, and musicianship in phrasing."

Though Thomas is one of our most admired operatic baritones, he greatly prefers the concert stage to the opera house. To a recital of songs he brings a charming informality, together with a lusty zest which betrays the inordi-

nate pleasure he derives from his job. Each year he gives
between sixty and seventy recitals, and often before immense audiences; at one concert in Chicago he sang before 100,000, while in Pittsburgh, 45,000 came to hear
him. Between March 1, 1947 and April 1948, he covered
40,000 miles in this country, giving 110 recitals. Then he
undertook the most intensive tour of Australia and New
Zealand attempted by an American artist, earning what is
surely an all-time record for that part of the world, the
equivalent of $250,000 (or an average of $5,000 a concert). His radio public, of course, is counted by the millions. And his large audiences never tire of him, of his
inimitable projection of the great songs of all nations.

In 1939–40, Thomas gave a series of recitals in New
York devoted to the songs of France, England, Italy, Germany, and the United States. His versatility, the flexibility
of his style, and the broad range of his musical intelligence
were never more in evidence than in this cycle. Thomas
proved then that he is equally at home in every branch of
song literature. But in the songs of America he is incomparable. The acclaim given him at the last of his concerts
in his series—the one devoted to the United States—convinced him that his public wants him to sing American
songs, and they have been featured prominently on his
programs ever since.

If Thomas had not become a celebrated singer he would
probably have won fame as a sportsman. In golf, his score
is in the neighborhood of 80; in tennis, he has been able
to give a good account of himself in contests with Bill
Tilden. He is quite expert at fishing (he has caught a
tarpon weighing 400 pounds) and at boating (he has established the famous Thomas Trophy for the American

Power Boat Association). In addition, he is more than passingly adept at boxing and playing baseball.

When he is free from the pressure of concert work, Thomas lives with his wife on a farm near Los Angeles. There he raises crops and livestock that make the place completely self-supporting. There is nothing he enjoys more than to wear dungarees and boots and plunge into the varied physical activities around a farm, such as chopping wood, pitching hay, or ploughing. On this farm, incidentally, is found a precious sanctuary for rare birds —little-known European and Asiatic specimens which Thomas has collected over the years.

Thomas and his wife are passionate lovers of boats. Thomas has built up a fleet which is among his proudest possessions: it includes a 101-foot yacht, "The Masquerader," an 85-foot yacht, "The Memory," runabouts, speedboats, a fishing skiff, and a rowing dinghy.

II

PIANISTS

◇◇

1. *Vladimir Horowitz*
2. *Artur Rubinstein*
3. *Josef Hofmann*
4. *Artur Schnabel*
5. *Alexander Brailowsky*
6. *Rudolf Serkin*
7. *Myra Hess*

Vladimir Horowitz

1

VLADIMIR HOROWITZ

◇◇

Wʜᴇɴ Iɢɴᴀᴢ Jᴀɴ Pᴀᴅᴇʀᴇᴡsᴋɪ died in 1941, some writers said that a great tradition of piano-playing had died with him—"the grand manner," that expansive style that sweeps an audience off its feet with majestic sound, that concerns itself not with miniatures or details but with the general effect of the whole: the tradition established by Liszt, Anton Rubinstein, Busoni, and the other keyboard giants of the late nineteenth century.

To a certain extent these writers were correct. The day of bravura playing is dying. But it is not yet dead—it still lives in the performances of pianists like Vladimir Horowitz and Artur Rubinstein.

It was the great French critic, Henry Prunières, who said of Horowitz that "one can only compare him to Busoni and Paderewski." Colossus of the keyboard, Horowitz is probably the most magnetic pianist of our time, endowed as he is with a technique that is so fabulous that it accomplishes every problem set before it with deceptive ease. It is no coincidence that Horowitz worships Franz Liszt more than any other musician of the past—that he actually has made something of a fetish of a Liszt portrait that he carries with him all the time and looks at for good luck just before he goes on the concert stage. For Liszt was perhaps the greatest pianistic virtuoso of all time, and Horowitz has faithfully followed in his footsteps.

Like the masters of preceding generations, Horowitz combines technique with temperament. In listening to him, one is always conscious that this is Horowitz playing. His identity is unmistakable. His personal color is spread with generous brush strokes across the canvas of his music. The Horowitz magnetism endows with sparkle everything he plays. A Horowitz performance enriches discriminating music-lovers, but it also saps their strength, often leaving them limp with spent emotions. For you cannot listen to Horowitz with dispassionate detachment. His personality is much too positive, too assertive, for that; its vibrancy charges the atmosphere, acting almost hypnotically upon the audience.

Actually, there have been two Horowitzes. One appeared until 1936; the second has emerged since then. The first was the prodigious technician who unfortunately made us continually conscious of his technical powers. Often there was beautiful playing; often an intelligent projection of the composer's intentions. Yet we could never quite lose our awareness of the means by which Horowitz arrived at his artistic ends—and to many this seemed to be Horowitz's artistic Achilles heel, his fatally vulnerable point as a great interpreter.

But in 1936, Horowitz—now famous throughout the world—went into a two-year retirement. Rumor had it that he was seriously ill, so ill that it was doubtful whether he would ever return to the concert stage. Actually, it was Horowitz's growing dissatisfaction with himself as an artist that had impelled him to close his career—temporarily at least. He had always been (he still is) one of the most fastidiously self-critical virtuosos alive. Before he is ready to present a composition, he again and again subjects his

performance to a microscopic analysis. Even then—though
he is rhapsodically praised for it by the critics—he is dis-
satisfied and proceeds at once to make further improve-
ments. This severe, relentless self-analysis drove him in
1936 to work over not only one work but his entire repertoire.

Three years before this he had married Wanda Toscanini, daughter of the great conductor, and it may be that
his intimate association with one of the most celebrated
musicians of our generation had given him a new purpose
and direction; it may even be that Toscanini urged him to
make some decisive move toward rehabilitating himself
artistically. In any case, Horowitz felt that the time had
come for renewed study, for getting a fresh perspective on
his career, for a complete renovation of his artistic values.
For two years he did not touch a piano. He rested a great
deal, studied musical scores a great deal, reflected a great
deal. "I think I really began to live then," he later explained in an interview. "For years I had been playing
constantly. . . . Actually I played certain works so often
that I couldn't hear them any more, even while my fingers
were performing them. . . . I think I grew as an artist, during this long vacation. At any rate, I think I found new
things in my music. I know that I learned more than I
could possibly have learned if I had been continuing the
exhausting rounds of practicing, rushing for trains, and
giving concerts month after month."

Out of this period of rest and study emerged a new
Vladimir Horowitz, still the greatest technician of his time,
but now a musician who had been spiritually enriched and
revitalized. A concert in Paris in 1939 proved to the world
that Horowitz had grown more sober, mellow, and mature; that if he could still be dazzlingly pyrotechnic in, say,
Liszt, he could also plumb profound emotional depths in

Beethoven. On January 31, 1940, Horowitz returned to Carnegie Hall. Since that time he has been, without question, one of the greatest box-office attractions among the virtuosos of our time. But what is even more important is the fact that it is since that second American début that he has proved once and for all his right to belong to that imperial line of great musicians that included Liszt, Busoni, Anton Rubinstein, and Paderewski.

The curious fact about Horowitz's amazing technique is that it has been acquired through the blood, sweat, and tears of hard practicing. His remarkable hands have such muscular flexibility that the keyboard offers them few problems that are not easily soluble. He confesses that he has not worked on scales or arpeggios since his fifteenth year; that during the past two decades his practice work did not require more than two or three hours a day, if that. This, of course, does not mean that he does not work hard at his music; work, to Horowitz, means studying musical scores, memorizing new ones, reanalyzing and rediscovering familiar ones. Before Horowitz adds a new piece of music by a comparatively unfamiliar composer to his repertoire, even if it is only a five-minute work, he must go through and analyze the entire piano literature of that composer, so that he can assimilate and understand all the facets of his personality. Nor does it mean that he does not play the piano during his leisure hours. He and his piano are often inseparable, and he is always performing at the slightest provocation or the faintest semblance of an invitation.

An exhausting concert season in the winter, and summer months of intensive score-reading and study, do not permit a very active social life, even if Horowitz wanted one—as he does not. Naturally shy, and something of a hypochondriac, he prefers the quiet of his own living room, surrounded by his scores, books and precious collection of modern paintings, to taxing social functions. When he seeks diversion he finds it in the movies—any kind of movies will do, for he is a rabid fan; in playing rummy or poker; in occasionally visiting some night spot to hear good "hot" jazz; in indulging in his favorite sports of mountain-climbing, motoring, or swimming; or in parlor conversation on art, politics, literature, current events. But his greatest pleasure is to entertain a small circle of close friends at his home, to play the piano for them, or to play chamber music—say with his lifelong friends Nathan Milstein and Gregor Piatigorsky.

His natural diffidence extends to the concert platform. Though he has made more than a thousand public appearances, he is still terrified by audiences, and before a concert he is as irritable and distraught as a novice. Once, as soloist with Toscanini, he was the victim of a particularly severe attack of nerves. He refused to play, saying he simply couldn't. The manager prevailed upon him at least to go out on the stage and explain to the audience that he would be unable to perform. Horowitz consented, went out, saw the audience, then resolutely walked to the piano—and performed.

Horowitz was born in Kiev on October 1, 1904, the son of a successful electrical engineer. His obvious aptitude for music, apparent from his earliest years, he inherited from his mother, a gifted pianist. In the Horowitz household good music was heard continually; all the Horowitz children were early taught to play and to listen. Vladimir began learning the elements of piano-playing when he was six years old. Six years later, he was enrolled in the Kiev Conservatory where his piano teacher was Felix Blumfeld (formerly a pupil of Anton Rubinstein). From that institution, he was graduated in his seventeenth year with the highest honors. It is interesting to remark that at this time Horowitz's ambition was to become a composer, and not a concert pianist.

In 1922, Vladimir's uncle, a music critic, arranged to have the boy make his official concert début—in Kharkov. That concert was a sensation; for days afterward the talk in music circles was of the young man's electrifying virtuosity. He had to give thirteen concerts in Kharkov, paid for his efforts not in coin (which in the early days of the revolution was scarce) but in food, clothing, household appliances. Horowitz was then engaged for seventy appearances in Russia, twenty-three of them in Leningrad alone. He played a different program for each concert, more than 200 compositions in all. In 1925, he toured Europe for the first time. Wherever he went he was a sensation. He appeared as soloist with the greatest orchestras of Europe and under its most famous conductors, and gave command performances before crowned heads. In short, he had arrived.

Artur Judson heard him play in Paris and signed him for an American tour. On January 12, 1928, he made his American début as soloist with the New York Philharmonic, playing the Tchaikovsky concerto under the direction of Sir Thomas Beecham. It was a breathtaking exhibition of virtuosity (though not a consistently sound musical exhibition), and the New York public was his. "It has been years," commented Olin Downes in the *New York Times,* "since a pianist created such a furor with an audience in this city. . . . His treatment of the work was a whirlwind of virtuoso interpretation. Mr. Horowitz has amazing strength, irresistible youth, and temperament."

No question of his instantaneous success! And with each succeeding season it kept growing. His rapidly expanding fame can best be measured by the yardstick of the fees he has commanded. In 1928 he earned only $500 a recital. In 1929, the fee jumped to $1,000, and in 1930 to $1,500. By 1930, he was filling a hundred engagements a season in America alone. Today, Horowitz is paid $3,000 a recital, and he can have as many appearances as he wishes; he limits his concert work, however, to no more than two appearances a week over a period of no more than six months; the rest of the time he must rest, study, subject himself to analysis.

In 1932, Arturo Toscanini conducted a Beethoven cycle with the New York Philharmonic. At the last concert of this series the *Emperor Concerto* was scheduled, and Horowitz was selected as the soloist. Conferences between Toscanini and Horowitz took place at the Maestro's suite at the Hotel Astor. It was not long before an intimate bond of friendship was established between the two musicians. The following summer, Horowitz was invited to Toscanini's home on Lake Maggiore in northern Italy. There he was treated as a member of the family—and he became a real member of the family a few months later when he married Toscanini's daughter, Wanda. The Horowitzes have one daughter, Sonia, who plays the piano moderately well (a Horowitz, one must confess, in name only), but whose special talent is painting.

ARTUR RUBINSTEIN

◇◇◇

ARTUR RUBINSTEIN bears one of the most hallowed names in the history of the piano, for Anton Rubinstein (no relative) was one of the foremost piano virtuosos of the nineteenth century. The later Rubinstein bears the name gracefully; more than that, he has brought to it additional honor. For, like his distinguished predecessor, he combines a prodigious technique with musicianship, scholarship, and a richly poetic temperament to a point where the music he interprets seems to be born anew under his fingertips. In Chopin, surely, he is today incomparable. No one since Paderewski has brought to Chopin's music such a wide gamut of color, mood, and atmosphere, or so successfully revealed his music to be the very lifeblood of Poland. But Rubinstein is by no means a one-composer specialist—poetic fire sets aflame his Beethoven, Brahms, Schumann, as well. In the music of the moderns, his playing is a galvanic force that moves with irresistible momentum. How highly he is esteemed by modern composers, many of whom regard him as their ideal interpreter, is demonstrated by the fact that nine of them have dedicated works to him: Stravinsky, Prokofiev, Szymanowski, Tansman, Villa-Lobos, Milhaud, Poulenc,

Artur Rubinstein

Ponce, and Carpenter. Surely his musical world is an expansive one!

His amazing technique and virtuosity—which, regrettably, he has in recent years made a *visual* as well as an *aural* experience for his audiences—have made him box-office magic. His fee, which is computed on a percentage basis, is the highest received by anybody in the concert field today, ranging from a minimum of $3,500 to as much as $5,500. Since he does not emulate Horowitz in rationing his concerts over a six-month period (he averages 150 concerts a year; and in the past eleven years he has made 814 appearances), his annual earnings from concert work alone are well over $350,000. To this figure must be added his royalties from recordings, which have been in the neighborhood of $100,000 a year (his albums of the Rachmaninoff Second and Grieg A minor concertos brought into the shops $1,000,000!). Besides, he gathers handsome fees for his appearances in motion pictures: in two films (*Carnegie Hall* and *Night Song*) he appeared on the screen, while in two others (*I've Always Loved You* and *Song of Love*) he merely recorded the piano selections on the sound track. For one of these assignments alone—his stint for *I've Always Loved You* which took him three days—he received $85,000.

He has had such a long and rich career that he may be considered a connecting link between two generations of piano-playing. He first became famous at the turn of the present century—a period that knew the fabulous art of Busoni, Tausig, Paderewski, Rosenthal, and the other gigantic figures of piano virtuosity; and even in such distinguished company he was by no means an artist to be ignored. Today—four decades later, in another age, and with other gods and traditions—he is still among the elect.

Artur Rubinstein was born in Lodz, Poland, in 1886, the youngest of seven children. At three, he began playing the piano, and at four he made his first public appearance—at a charity concert in his native town. Four years later he became a pupil of Prof. Rozycki, who soon became so impressed by the boy's natural aptitude for the piano that he arranged to have Joseph Joachim hear him. At the time, Joachim was one of the most notable musicians in Europe—world-famous as a violinist, almost as celebrated with the baton, and the friend of Brahms and Schumann when those composers were alive. Joachim, therefore, was not without influence. After hearing the boy play, he proceeded to put that influence to work on behalf of the prodigy. He assumed personal responsibility for the boy (which he carried for eight years), and arranged to have Rubinstein continue his musical study in Berlin with Heinrich Barth, Robert Kahn, and Max Bruch. Then, in 1897, he set the stage for Rubinstein's formal début as a concert artist, having Artur appear under his baton in Berlin in a performance of the Mozart A major concerto.

When he was thirteen, Rubinstein appeared as soloist with the Warsaw Philharmonic, then conducted by Emil Mlynarski. (Many years later, Rubinstein married Mlynarski's daughter.) Soon after this, Serge Koussevitzky invited Rubinstein to accompany him and his orchestra on an extended tour of Russia.

Wherever he went, he attracted attention and praise—not only from the public but even from established musicians. Paderewski was so enchanted by his playing that he had the boy live with him for three months so that they might work together at the piano. In Paris, Saint-Saëns referred to him as "one of the greatest artists I know."

In January, 1906, Rubinstein made his American début, appearing as soloist with the Philadelphia Orchestra in a performance of Chopin's E minor concerto. Seventy-five concerts carried him from one end of the country to the other, and when the tour ended, his reputation was firmly established. It was then that Rubinstein made a brave decision. Though his success was now assured and a profitable career was now within his grasp, he suddenly decided to withdraw from all concert work; he realized the need of further study, both musical and academic. Success, he felt, would be hollow if he did not feel himself worthy of it. For several years, therefore, he worked hard and studied, far from the limelight, to hurdle (as he himself put it) "the greatest obstacle in the path of a prodigy, that of shedding immaturity." In that time a phenomenal prodigy ripened into a profound artist.

He emerged from his period of study and retirement to concertize extensively throughout all of Europe and to receive that acclaim which his mastery deserved. By the time war broke out in Europe in 1914 he had played in its major cities. In London when war came, he presented himself to the Polish legation as a volunteer for the Polish legion. At first, his linguistic talents were exploited; then his musical genius. He gave a series of thirty concerts with Eugène Ysaÿe for the Allied forces. A personal witness of the brutality inflicted by German soldiers on civilians, the experience so revolted him that he made a personal vow never to appear in Germany, a vow he kept for more than three decades.

In 1916, he visited Spain for the first time, scheduled to give four concerts but compelled by his phenomenal success to give 120! His sympathy for the country, its people, and its music, and his intimate association with its foremost composers, has since that year made him a particularly brilliant interpreter of contemporary Spanish music, a fact that the Spanish themselves have long come to recognize and appreciate. From Spain he went on for an extensive tour of South America.

Then in 1919, Rubinstein returned to the United States. On February 20, 1919, he gave a recital at Carnegie Hall, his first appearance in this country in more than a decade. The audience, and the critics, were his. "Rubinstein's finger velocity, staccato, brilliant and incisive, with a splendid left hand, are undeniable qualities," reported James Gibbons Huneker, "coupled with a sweet singing touch and a musical temperament—in all, traits sufficient to equip a half-dozen artists."

Since that time, Rubinstein has been accepted everywhere as one of the great piano virtuosos of our generation. After concertizing here for many years, he concentrated his concert activity in the European capitals for a ten-year period. In 1937, he reappeared in this country for a third time, once again after an absence of about a decade. And once again his successes here were decisive. He has subsequently become an American citizen and transferred his permanent home from Paris to the outskirts of Los Angeles. With the lion's share of his concert work belonging to our auditoriums, he occupies a niche all his own in our musical life.

His home near Los Angeles is the thirty-second he has had in many different parts of the world. Though Rubinstein is inordinately proud of his American citizenship, and always considers himself an American, he is essentially an internationalist. The influence of more than 2,000,000 miles of travel around the world is ineradicable. He speaks nine languages fluently; when, in his living room, he entertains his many friends of many different countries, it is not unusual to find him shifting from one language to another as he passes from one friend to the next. His dinner table is as international as his living room. A renowned gourmet, Rubinstein has brought the delicacies and succulent recipes of Europe and the Orient to his kitchen. Even his family itself reflects to a degree this international tendency. He, himself, is of Polish birth; his wife, though of Polish origin, is American. They were married in London. Their first child, Eva, was born in Buenos Aires in 1933; their second, Paul, in Warsaw in 1935; their third and fourth, Alice and Arthur, in Hollywood, in 1945 and 1946 respectively.

Immensely cultured, a fascinating conversationalist, and a much-quoted wit, Rubinstein goes in for physical and intellectual pleasures, and with equal measure. He is as fond of good food, good drink, good Havana cigars, as he is of books and paintings (of which he has valuable collections) and parlor discussions. His is an exceptional zest for the good things of life. As he once put it: "There is no *ersatz* for living. I prefer to die young than to sniff around life. People go to doctors and ask: 'What vitamins shall I eat?' I ask you—what good are vitamins? Eat *four* lobsters. Eat a pound of caviar. *Live!* If you are in love with a beautiful blonde, don't be afraid, and don't think too much. Marry her!" He has many and varied interests (politics, the genealogy of European nobility, Hindu sculpture) but he adds roguishly that "of all my interests, 90% are women."

At the present time, one extra-curricular activity engages his energy and enthusiasm more than any other: the Frederic Chopin Fund which he founded late in 1946 and of which he is president. Recognizing the dire needs of professional musicians in post-war Europe, Rubinstein created the Fund to provide needy European musicians with whatever books, scores, musical instruments or other tools of their trade they need in order to rehabilitate themselves professionally.

3

JOSEF HOFMANN

◇◇◇

Wㅤ H E N, on the evening of November 28, 1937, Josef
Hofmann gave his Golden Jubilee concert at the Metropolitan Opera House, there must have been more than one
in the audience whose memory could reach back fifty
years. Then, in that very same hall, Hofmann had made
his American début—a child prodigy. That début had
been one of the great events, not only in the musical but
also in the social life of New York during the closing
decades of the nineteenth century. He was, at the time,
eleven years old. His early photographs revealed a round
face with small features, his closely cropped hair encircling
his head like a tight skullcap. His nose was turned slightly
upwards over lips that were thin and fine; his eyes were
soft and sensitive; his hands, small but strong. His chubby
cheeks radiated health, while his body showed muscle and
sinew.

He had come to America preceded by news of an almost
incredible career, a career extravagantly discussed in the
newspapers and magazines before his arrival, and talked
about over teacups and liquor glasses in the nation's living
rooms. He was the "musical phenomenon" that Anton
Rubinstein had called him.

His life story, brief though it was at the time, had been

well known before he arrived: how into ten short years he
had crowded enough triumph to enrich many a full life's
span. Born in Kracow, Poland, on January 20, 1876, he
was the child of musical parents: his mother was an operatic soprano of some renown; his father Casimir, a composer, pianist, and a conductor at the Warsaw Opera. Already at the age of three and a half, Josef played the
piano, taught first by his little sister, a year and a half
his senior. Josef learned his exercises with lightning rapidity. He passed from the instruction of his sister to that of
his aunt; and one year later—because his aunt could teach
him no more—he became a pupil of his father.

A little more than a year after he had first touched the
piano, Josef made his professional début in a suburb of
Warsaw. It was considered by many so sensational a first
performance that a deluge of offers descended upon Casimir Hofmann to have his son concertize. Wisely, Father
Hofmann refused to exploit the child. He permitted only
a scattered handful of concerts, all for charity—carefully
spaced to spare Josef's strength. These concerts spread the
boy's reputation throughout Poland.

When he was seven years old, Josef played the first
movement of Beethoven's first piano concerto with what
the critics referred to as an instinctive feeling for the style
of the composer, precision, and a full, round, singing tone.
It was at about this time that Anton Rubinstein first heard
him play, in Warsaw. The performance stirred the master
profoundly, and he mentioned the prodigy to the German
impresario, Hermann Wolf, suggesting concert appearances. How deeply Rubinstein had been moved by Hofmann's playing became even more evident a few months
later in London. A friend of Rubinstein broached the subject of child prodigies, and Rubinstein said that he had
little taste for them. There was only one exception, the

master said, whose equal the history of music would surely fail to duplicate. "And the name of the scoundrel," said Rubinstein, as he struck several powerful chords on the piano, "is Josef Hofmann!"

As a consequence of Rubinstein's enthusiasm, Wolf persistently urged Casimir Hofmann to permit concert engagements for the boy. The world of music, he argued, must hear him. When Josef was ten years old, Father Hofmann yielded to the entreaties of the manager. Hofmann's first concert outside of Poland was in Berlin, at one of the symphony concerts of the Berlin Philharmonic, when he played the complete first piano concerto of Beethoven. His concert was a triumph; the audience cheered its appreciation wildly after the performance. But the members of the orchestra itself had expected as much, for at the first rehearsal they had seen the child Josef pulling at the coat of the conductor, Prof. Manstadt, to tell him that the violoncellos were not playing correctly in one passage— a defect that few of the other musicians had noticed!

Appearances followed in Denmark, Sweden, Norway, and Holland. Then Hofmann went to Paris, where Saint-Saëns exclaimed that this phenomenon had nothing more to learn, that he was "the greatest wonder of the present age."

With all this America was well acquainted; long before his much-heralded début in the United States, his exploits were repeatedly recorded in the press. "For nearly four years he has been appearing before the public as a piano virtuoso," wrote *Harper's Young People* in 1887, comparing Hofmann to Mozart in an earlier paragraph, "and lately he has appeared very frequently, and created what the newspapers call a 'sensation.' Never was so much written about a young man by his contemporaries as has been written about this young Hofmann. Famous musicians

Alexander Brailowsky

like Rubinstein, and callous old critics like—well, most of
the famous ones—have fairly gushed over him. It is a wonder that with all the attention he has received, the little
fellow has not become very conceited. . . . Away from
music, he is always a child, and his sense of humor is delightful. One day, his parents promised to pay him twenty-
five cents for each concert, and, subsequently, when he
finished a concert and encores were demanded, he said:
'No,' with a merry laugh, 'the concert is over and I have
earned my quarter.' But he played encores, and upon returning to the artists' room said, 'Now, in the future, you
must pay me by the piece—two cents for my own compositions, and five cents for the others.' "

When Josef Hofmann stepped on the stage of the Metropolitan Opera House on November 29, 1887—performing
the first piano concerto of Beethoven, the *Variations* by
Rameau, a *Polacca* by Weber-Liszt, a set of pieces by
Chopin and one of his own creations—the atmosphere was
charged with expectancy. A thundering ovation wel-
comed him as he stepped on the platform, dressed in a
striped sailor shirt and knee breeches—a pretty sight for
the eye. Then, with poise and self-assurance, he climbed
to the stool, ran his fingers casually over the keys, and
patiently waited for the whispers and exclamations of the
audience to subside. Only when an intense silence prevailed did he signal to the conductor to begin the opening
bars of the concerto. Then he played. "When he con-
cluded the Beethoven concerto," reported W. J. Henderson the following morning in the *New York Times,* "a
thunder of applause swept through the opera house. Many
people leaped to their feet. Men shouted 'Bravo!' and
women waved their handkerchiefs. Pianists of repute were
moved almost to tears. Some wiped the moisture from their
eyes. The child had astonished the assembly. He was a

marvel. The second movement of the Beethoven concerto was performed in a manner that startled experienced observers of musical events. The first movement had been played with wonderful refinement of touch, with a complete mastery of technical difficulties, with rich and varied tone-color, and with surprising brilliancy in the treatment of the difficult Moscheles cadenza. But in the second movement there was no room for imposition on the senses through the medium of ornamental passages. The pure and elevated melody stood forth in unclothed beauty, and could only be adequately interpreted by an artist. Josef Hofmann played, not only like an artist, but like a master. The tenderness of sentiment, the poetic insight into the meaning, the symmetrical conception of the movement as a whole, and the ability to make the music not only arouse the intelligence but move the heart of the hearer, as displayed by this child, were simply wonderful. . . . The feeling and intelligence shown by young Hofmann in this movement were far and away beyond his years. They showed that he was a born musician—that rare thing which the world always hungers for and greets with affectionate veneration. Suffice it to say, for the present, that Josef Hofmann, as a musical phenomenon, is worthy of the sensation which he created. More than that, he is an artist, and we can listen to his music without taking into consideration the fact that he is a child."

The memory of many in the audience which heard Josef Hofmann's Golden Jubilee concert in 1937 must also have brought back to mind vividly an evening eleven years after the début—in 1898—when Hofmann, no longer the child prodigy but now the mature artist, made his American reappearance as a concert pianist, his first appearance in America since his childhood. He had recently emerged from a long period of retirement, which had been devoted to intensive study. After his phenomenal American début at the Metropolitan Opera House, Hofmann gave sixteen additional concerts at the Metropolitan and twenty-four on tour. Then the Society for Prevention of Cruelty to Children, of New York, objected to Hofmann's extensive concert work as detrimental to his health and growth, and pressed for removing him from active concertizing. The pressure was effective: though Hofmann was booked for eighty engagements in America that year, he was suddenly retired. An anonymous patron appeared (later identified as Alfred Corning Clark of New York) who offered to provide financially for the child and his family until Josef should reach his eighteenth birthday, on condition that he be kept off the concert stage and devote himself to study and relaxation.

During the long period that followed, young Hofmann was given thorough and comprehensive schooling, not only in music but in academic subjects as well. The family returned to Europe, where the study of musical theory and composition was pursued under Heinrich Urban, and the piano first under Casimir Hofmann and then under Moritz Moszkowski. Moszkowski was no less enthusiastic about his pupil than other teachers had been. "The boy knows so much," he once said, "and plays so much better than I do, that I don't know how to teach him."

When Josef Hofmann reached his sixteenth birthday, he became the only private pupil of Anton Rubinstein. He had long wished to study under Rubinstein, but the master—despite his one-time enthusiasm for Hofmann's genius—remained obstinate in his refusal to accept private pupils. At a party in Berlin which was given by the impresario Hermann Wolf and at which Rubinstein was a guest, Hofmann was invited to play. He performed his own *Theme, Variations and Fugue,* Opus 14. After the performance Rubinstein approached him. "You may not be a pianist yet," he said, "but you are certainly a musician." Lukewarm praise, it seemed; but how deeply Rubinstein had been moved by Hofmann's music was forcibly demonstrated then and there when the master decided to accept Hofmann as his only private pupil.

Teaching Hofmann was an experience for Rubinstein which brought with it renewed reward and cause for wonder; he never wearied in relating the wonders of his phenomenal pupil. "He is," said the master—who was never careless with superlatives, particularly where the playing of the piano was concerned—"the greatest genius of music the world has ever known."

One day (Hofmann had by this time been Rubinstein's pupil for two years) the master called his pupil and ordered him to commit to memory and prepare for concert performance within two days Rubinstein's own Concerto in D minor. Hofmann, terrified, exclaimed that two days was too short a time for such a formidable assignment. "Formidable?" answered Rubinstein. "There is *nothing* formidable for *us!*"

Two days later Hofmann had learned the concerto, and that very evening at a symphony concert in Hamburg he made his first appearance on the concert stage in seven years. At the end of the performance, Rubinstein rushed to the stage and threw his huge arms about his pupil. For that performance had proved to Rubinstein that Hofmann was in consummate command of all the resources of the piano, that he had become a mature and profound artist, prepared for his life as a concert pianist.

Six months later, in the autumn of 1894, a new tour was launched by Hofmann, first in England (where his audience included his benefactor, Alfred Corning Clark, who had come from America expressly to attend that performance), and then in Germany and Russia. In 1898, Hofmann crossed the Atlantic westwards for the second time and, in a tour that took him from one coast to another, demonstrated eloquently to audiences that crowded the concert halls to the doors that the one-time prodigy had grown into one of the great artists of his time.

Meanwhile, Hofmann had said permanent farewell to his master Rubinstein, who had had such a profound influence upon his artistic growth. Their last musical association had taken place in Hamburg in March of 1894, when Hofmann played the Rubinstein D minor Concerto with the composer conducting. A few weeks later—following a Rubinstein concert in Leipzig which Hofmann attended—a social tea brought teacher and pupil together for the last time. "When will you listen to me play again?" Hofmann asked Rubinstein. "Never again!" bellowed the great Russian master. "I have taught you all I know myself about piano playing. If you do not know how to play yet, you can go to hell!"

Hofmann was never again to play for his teacher. On November 19, 1894, as Hofmann was on his way from London to Cheltenham, a newspaper headline told him that Rubinstein was dead. "It seemed to me that I had lost not only my greatest benefactor but also the dearest person on earth, for not only did I admire him—I had grown to love him as well."

By a curious coincidence, Hofmann was scheduled to play that evening, at the concert in Cheltenham, the great B-flat minor Sonata of Chopin, with the funeral march. That evening he played the funeral march, not for his audience, but for the great master who had died that day. Never before, and perhaps never since, had he so poured his heart into this music which was his tribute to Rubinstein. The audience must have sensed the significance of

Hofmann's performance, for one by one they stood up as he played on, and during the closing page they were all on their feet, heads bowed reverently, paying their own last tribute to Rubinstein.

Hofmann has enriched the art of music through more than one channel. He has been a composer of many works which, if not of Gargantuan stature, are not by any means insignificant. Until 1922, he disguised his work—created in the modern vein—under the pseudonym of "Michael Dvorsky" so that his enormous fame as a virtuoso might not influence the music world on behalf of his creations. For years, "Michael Dvorksy"—the ghost of Hofmann—haunted the concert halls. Piano pieces signed with this unknown name were introduced at recitals by leading virtuosos; a symphonic poem and other larger compositions for orchestra, or orchestra and piano, were performed by symphony organizations. And for years the world at large remained ignorant of the true identity of Dvorsky. It was rumored that he was a new Russian composer residing in Spain; beyond that, nothing was known. Finally Hofmann revealed himself. As though to celebrate the revelation, an entire Josef Hofmann program was featured by the Philadelphia Orchestra on January 2, 1924. It included the symphonic poem *The Haunted Castle,* the second Concerto for piano and orchestra, and *Chromaticon,* a "symphonic dialogue for piano and orchestra."

Even more significant has been Hofmann's rôle as a teacher. In 1926, he was appointed the director of the Curtis Institute of Music in Philadelphia. During the twelve years in which he directed one of the great conservatories in this country, his influence was felt by a rising generation of young pianists. Unfortunately, in 1938,

Hofmann decided that his day as a teacher and director was over. His withdrawal as director of the Curtis removed one of the major musical influences in our country.

Yet—distinguished though his work as composer and teacher may be—his greatest importance lies in his piano playing. It is, indeed, regrettable that in recent years his performances should have been so few and far between. But the memory of his playing remains vivid even to those who have not heard him for a while. So much has been written about his technical capacities that detailed comment should be unnecessary here. Certainly, his digital equipment for the piano is breath-taking: his complete control of all the resources of the piano, from the sensitivity of whispering voices to the full-throated sonority of orchestral chords. Certainly, few in our time can enunciate, as Hofmann can, scale passages with such crystalline clarity, cleanness, and despatch; and few have his remarkably infallible instinct for the rhythmic beat. Certainly, too, few pianists of our experience can convert the piano into such a choir of singing strings as Hofmann can: his tone has depth and roundness, intensity and warmth, variety of color, delicacy of tints. He is the complete master of the keyboard; the instrument is utterly at his command, and at his hands all music is immaculately, perfectly conceived.

This phenomenal command of his instrument Hofmann had when Rubinstein praised him, and this phenomenal command he still possesses. And along with this equipment, which some go so far as to say is without parallel in our time, he brings to the performance of certain works a fullness of heart, a breadth of conception, a living force, a windswept emotion, a beauty of design and expression, which make him one of the great interpreters of our generation.

The critics have often commented on the eternal youth in Hofmann's playing. Youth, indeed—for youth has never forsaken Hofmann himself. The exhausting and strenuous life of a world-famous concert artist has imposed small penalty on him. The average concert artist, after passing his sixtieth birthday, looks aged, as though his energies were sapped; his physical appearance shows the strain of endless travel and concert appearances. But there is still something remarkably youthful and fresh about Hofmann.

He has even retained remarkably the features of his boyhood: the round face and chubby cheeks, the closely cropped hair, the upturned nose, the small, powerful hands. His skin is still soft and supple, and noticeably free of the lines and creases of age; wrinkles on his face appear only when he smiles—short lines that radiate from his eyes, giving his face not a little of its engaging charm. And he has retained not only the features but even the extraordinary energy and health of his youth. Today he appears amazingly vital. Athletics—boating and hiking, particularly—have kept his body resilient and strong. When he shakes your hand, it is with a firm, strong grasp. His gestures, which are frequent, are animated. When he talks, it is always volubly and energetically (his conversation liberally studded with epigrams), and so zestfully that, after a few sentences, he must stop for a fraction of a second to moisten his lips with the tip of his tongue, which he does with flashing rapidity.

An amazing variety of interests has kept his spirit as vigorous and young as his body. Music is only one element in a well-proportioned existence; it has not interfered with an intelligent and satisfying home life. Hofmann, in spite of extensive concert tours, lives a very retired domestic life at his spacious home in Merion, Pennsylvania, where he spends the greater part of the year with his wife and three sons. Here he finds relaxation in playing ping-pong, rummy or chess with his boys. Here, too, he absorbs himself in his one major hobby, which has fascinated him since boyhood—invention and mechanics. When, as a boy, he was forbidden by his mother to ice-skate, he invented a collapsible set of skates which he could conceal in his pockets until he had passed out of his mother's sight. Since that time, he has spent endless hours in the laboratory translating what might first have appeared as fantastic dreams into practical realities. He was the first to design a model house whose foundation can rotate with the sun. When steam automobiles came into use, Hofmann built one for himself which he used for his personal transportation around the country. The oil-burning furnace in his home was designed and built by him. He has also invented, and built, automobile air-springs, shock-absorbers, and snubbers. To cope with warped floors on concert platforms which make the piano bench wobble, he has invented a collapsible bench whose legs can be adjusted individually to conform to the irregularities in the floor boards.

Where music is concerned, his tastes are amazingly conservative. He has little taste for the modern or the experimental in present-day music, and his programs eschew the new and unfamiliar. A Hofmann recital is, for the most part, a journey along familiar trails—familiar trails on which he points out for us new and subtle beauties in the landscape that had formerly eluded us. He has a phenomenal memory for music, can almost impress upon his mind an entire composition after one hearing. Pupils of his have been astounded when, having played for him one of their own compositions, they then hear Hofmann, without consulting the music, play one passage after another exactly as it was put on paper.

Such a phenomenal memory naturally reduces the hours

needed for practicing at a keyboard. Hofmann practices while lounging in a soft chair, while sprawling in a hammock, while taking walks in the woods, or while riding in trains. He closes his eyes, relaxes, appears to be asleep; but he is, in fact, going over every note, and every nuance, of an entire program. Shortly before a concert, he translates this mental practicing into actual tones at the piano, but only after his conception of the music has been clearly and forcefully impressed on his mind. He does not recommend this method for every pianist; it requires an enormous capacity for concentration, a prodigious memory, and a complete confidence in one's technical facility.

Artur Schnabel

4

ARTUR SCHNABEL

◇◇◇

O N F O U R different occasions Artur Schnabel has
given a comprehensive cycle of concerts devoted to the
thirty-two piano sonatas of Beethoven—twice in Berlin,
once in London, and once in New York. He has recorded
all the Beethoven piano sonatas on phonograph records,
and has edited and annotated an edition of these sonatas.
He has also recorded all the five piano concertos of the
master, as well as the *Diabelli Variations*. Finally, Beethoven's music has almost inevitably appeared on his programs during the span of his career. He therefore handsomely deserves the designation often given him by critics
—"Beethoven's high-priest."

Schnabel realizes that it is a shortcoming in an interpreter to devote himself so completely to the music of any
one composer. "Make no mistake," he once said, not without a slight touch of irony; "it is my limitation that I play
so much Beethoven. But I am completely happy in my
one-sidedness."

But Schnabel need make no apologies for his artistic
devotion to Beethoven. For one thing, the piano music of
Beethoven (and this is, I think, truer of his works than of
the piano works of any other composer, even J. S. Bach)
embraces so many different styles, so many diverse mes-

sages, such a variety of mood and atmosphere, that a great interpreter of these sonatas must have the plasticity of approach and technique required for the interpretation of music by many different composers. From the classicism of Opus 2 to the symphonic dynamics of Opus 111 there lies a mighty expanse, which no interpreter need be ashamed of claiming as his entire world.

Besides, Schnabel's artistic career has not been quite so one-sided as some have claimed. True, a Schnabel program usually ranges less widely than the programs of other pianists. He is sparing with Chopin, Liszt, Debussy—if he plays these composers at all. And, particularly during the past twenty years, he has not featured the music of modern composers. Schnabel is no enemy of modern music. As a matter of fact, two of the foremost living modernists, Paul Hindemith and Arnold Schoenberg, are his personal friends. And—curious to record!—in his own compositions Schnabel is brazenly audacious in his use of harmonic combinations. But, being a severely honest artist, he refuses to play any music that does not move him profoundly. "An artist," he has said, "should and does choose to play only that music of which he is particularly fond. And the field of what he likes should be wide enough."

As a matter of fact, Schnabel's own field of preferences *is* wide enough. He has played Mozart often—and beautifully. For Bach's music he has a decided liking, and he gives it all the breadth of design and proportion it requires. For a long time he was considered by many in Europe one of the greatest living interpreters of the piano music of Johannes Brahms. His Schubert (above all) has warmth, tenderness, an exquisite delicacy; many critics put it even above his Beethoven. When he plays Schumann, he discloses a profound insight into the pianistic style and musical content of the great Romanticist. With these composers, he feels, his artistic life is complete. "No matter how long my life is, it will be too short to get through Bach, Mozart, Beethoven, Schubert, Schumann, and Brahms. There is a necessity in me to play these composers."

Schnabel has, in some quarters, been even more frequently criticized for what is termed his "austere intellectualism" as a pianist—and with even less justification. He is intellectual, if by that word we imply the ability to analyze a musical work profoundly, and to reveal the fruits of this painstaking analysis in a performance. He is an intellectual, too, if that word is to be applied loosely to musicians who adhere meticulously to the printed wish of the composer. But there is nothing cut-and-dried about Schnabel's performances. They are, by no means, overcerebralized, or lacking in emotion. Schnabel is not one to yield to emotional excess, to make music—so to speak—the refuse place for his emotions. But his playing is always full of feeling, always moving. One has merely to recall his playing of the *Hammerklavier* Sonata of Beethoven in which, for example, the bizarre series of trills in the last movement, the noble resignation of the slow movement, the iron-fisted defiance of the opening chords, receive, at his hands, a performance blending poignancy and power. One has merely to recall the youthfulness with which he endows the Schubert B-flat major (posthumous) Sonata, or the emotional storms that sweep through his rendition of the Brahms B-flat major Concerto.

Schnabel, the pedant—the emotionally sterile intellectual? Absurd. He himself has often spoken eloquently on behalf of a greater emotional approach to music. "I assure you," he has said in an interview—a message he has repeated in more than one form—"that it is only when I forget my craftsmanship that I begin to enjoy music. . . . If

you want to learn all you can about music, that is splendid. But if you think that by learning you can make yourself love music, you are very much mistaken. . . . You do
not have to be a botanist to enjoy flowers growing in a
meadow. All this emphasis on learning and understanding
music! Music should not be learned and understood half
so much as it should be loved and enjoyed. One can understand it through love."

But why do we need his words, when his own playing
has said this so unmistakably?

Though in certain quarters Schnabel has been thus criticized—as we have shown, unjustifiably—his importance as
an interpreter is rarely questioned. That he is one of the
great pianists of our time, and one of the greatest living
interpreters of Beethoven, is generally conceded. His success in this country was not immediate, however; his art to
many appeared unsensational, his personality without magnetism. "A number of people," he has written, "immediately tried to give me a prescription on how to change
from the type of musician I consider myself—and am—into
some allegedly more popular king. I remember my manager telling me, 'Now listen, Mr. Schnabel, you have to be
sensible. When you come here, you have, let us say, ten
qualities. It will be enough to use only five of them and
we'll make a lot of money. We'll store the other five
qualities, and when you go back you can take out those
and use ten again." I took these things very seriously at
this time, so I said, 'You're mistaken. If I really have ten
qualities, as you say, the only tasks which attract me are
those requiring fifteen qualities.' But he only looked
blank."

He came to America for the first time in 1922. Yet,
though he played then quite as magnificently as he does
today, he was received coldly and apathetically. One rea-

son perhaps was the fact that, though he enjoyed at the time a solid reputation in Europe, his career offered little dramatic material, little with which to inflame the imagination of a virtuoso-crazy public.

He was born in Lipnik, Austria, on April 17, 1882, and began the study of music at an early age. At seven he was the pupil of Hans Schmitt. His progress was so rapid that when he was eight years old he made several successful concert appearances. It was decided to give him the best instruction in Vienna. In 1891, he became a pupil of the great Leschetizky, the teacher of Paderewski; his fellow pupils at the time included Ossip Gabrilowitsch and Mark Hambourg. In Leschetizky's famous house on the Carl Ludwigstrasse, Schnabel breathed a musical atmosphere. The most famous musicians of Vienna came to Leschetizky's to hear his pupils play, among them Johannes Brahms, Ignaz Brüll, Karl Goldmark, and the visiting Anton Rubinstein. Brahms heard Schnabel play one day, accosted him, and exclaimed: "How in the name of heaven can you play all this so correctly?"

Schnabel remained Leschetizky's pupil for six years. Then his concert life began. What followed—the slow and inevitable growth of an artist—was undramatic. He gave sonata recitals with the late Carl Flesch, violinist, and joint recitals with his wife, Therese Behr, an extraordinary Lieder singer; he played in trios. He gave piano recitals in Berlin. His fine musicianship was praised everywhere, and his reputation grew rapidly. Concert tours followed throughout Europe, his performances of Beethoven and Brahms being especially acclaimed. He appeared as soloist with the leading European orchestras, and under the batons of the foremost conductors, in concertos of Mozart, Beethoven, and Brahms. Following World War I, he was generally recognized as one of the foremost European pianists. In 1919 he was given the Honorary Professor degree by the Prussian State.

If in 1922, to New York music audiences, his background was unspectacular, what could one say then about his personality? When he stepped on the stage he seemed more like the successful businessman than the great artist. No lithe or supple lines of the body, no romantic shock of hair, no poetic expression. He was short and stockily built. His head, large and well formed, was covered with closely cropped, bristling hair. A mustache, thick as a brush, accentuated the full roundness of his face. Assuredly, an unromantic figure! Even his manner at the piano was anything but captivating. He played without flourishes, with no extravagant movements of the body. He played with despatch—played like a man who knows his business and can attend to it efficiently.

The New York music audiences that year liked to apotheosize their concert artists, and they did not take to Schnabel. He toured the country; toured again the following year; then, disappointed, resumed his concert career in Europe (where he was being appreciated more and more) and devoted himself industriously to teaching the piano. For many years he was the leader of a master class at the Prussian State Academy of Music.

It was seven years before he returned to America, where he had experienced perhaps the greatest failure of his career. But, at the insistence of his personal friends and pupils, he returned—a little more than a decade after his first visit. He found that the musical life in America had changed radically. "America seems to have reached maturity," he said. "It has slowly left the pioneering stage and the mass-production era. New artistic and spiritual things may be enjoyed more and more." The emphasis now was not on the virtuoso but on his playing; the American public had outgrown its fad for romantic concert artists. What it demanded now was great performances, and, moreover, great music. Into this scheme of things, Schnabel could fit harmoniously.

His success in America was soon established. This was proved eloquently in 1935 when he gave his monumental cycle of the Beethoven piano sonatas at Carnegie Hall. At first his managers tried to discourage him from the ambitious undertaking, fearing that the response would be unsatisfactory. But Schnabel had faith that New York was ripe for the venture—and his faith was justified: eighteen thousand people attended the seven concerts of Beethoven's sonatas, paying more than $23,000.

5

ALEXANDER BRAILOWSKY

❖❖

In The same way that Artur Schnabel is identified with Beethoven, so the art of Brailowsky is inevitably associated with the music of Frédéric Chopin.

His rich and successful career as pianist has long ago proved that Brailowsky (like Schnabel) can play many different styles well. Some years ago, he gave a series of twelve concerts in Buenos Aires in which he did not repeat a single work, and which wandered freely through the history of music from Johann Sebastian Bach to the modern composers. This, surely, is proof—if proof is needed—that his repertoire is not a limited one. François Plantet, the French musicologist, has spoken of Brailowsky as the "ideal Schumann interpreter"; the celebrated French musician, Camille Chevillard, pronounced him one of the great performers of Beethoven; and there are many critics in America who think that he is even more effective in modern works than in Chopin. Indeed (and this may come as a shock to some) Chopin is not even his favorite composer; he is much more sympathetic to Beethoven and Mozart.

Yet the public, when it comes to hear Brailowsky play, wants to hear him do Chopin. And, as a result, he plays Chopin frequently. In the past twenty-two years or so he has given his monumental cycle of six concerts devoted to

all the 169 solo works of Chopin thirteen times: four times
in Paris, three times in New York, twice in Buenos Aires,
and once each in Brussels, Montevideo, Zurich and Mexico
City.

He performed this series for the first time in Paris in
1924. All of the preceding summer he spent in seclusion
in the French Alps town of Annecy, working intensively
on the six programs. He catalogued the 169 works on separate cards, then spent eight weeks shifting the cards
around until he arrived at a convenient arrangement of
the various pieces. "To compile these six programs," he
has said, "was a task requiring many and varied considera-
tions. They had to be arranged in such a way that they
would not be monotonous—not too many mazurkas on one
program or too many waltzes on another. There had to be
variety of rhythms, colors, character, and length. Often I
spent hours trying to decide if a certain étude should go
before a mazurka or after it, or whether one sonata went
better with a certain work than with another. I worked as
though I were putting a big puzzle together. I think I
pulled each program apart twenty or thirty times before I
was satisfied with it." Parenthetically, the arrangement he
finally decided upon for the Paris concerts by no means
remained the definitive one. He has since that time changed
the position of the pieces to arrive at an ever happier combination.

The initial series—undertaken with no little trepidation,
since it was felt that there was no large audience for such
a comprehensive survey—proved so successful and turned
away so many disappointed music lovers who could not
gain admission that, on the evening of the last concert,
the manager announced the series would be repeated in a
larger auditorium. That second series sold out completely;
and Brailowsky's Chopin cycle has since been phenomen-

ally successful wherever he has undertaken it. At the
Teatro Colon in Buenos Aires a capacity audience of 4,000
attended each one of the concerts. In New York City, in
the 1946-47 series (the third time it was performed in this
city), 20,500 music lovers established what is considered a
box-office record at Carnegie Hall.

If Brailowsky thus taxes the seating capacity of every
hall in which he plays Chopin, it is because (as the critic
of the New York *Times* wrote) he "has this music in his
blood and conveys it with integrity and stirring convic-
tion." Those whose memories reach back many years maintain that Vladimir de Pachmann's performance of Chopin
was more sensitive than Brailowsky's, and Paderewski's,
more dramatic. But in Brailowskys' playing there is an
alluring blend of masculine virility and poetic refinement
which places his interpretations in their own class.

He was born on February 16, 1896 in Kiev, South
Russia, where his father was a piano teacher and the pro-
prietor of a music shop. From his father, Alexander received his first piano lessons, making such phenomenal
progress that when Rachmaninoff heard him play he said
grimly, "You are destined to be a great pianist." Several
wealthy members of the family arranged to bring the
Brailowskys to Vienna in 1911 so that Alexander might
study with Leschetizky. Leschetizky thought highly of Alexander (Brailowsky was destined to be the last of the master's celebrated pupils), and before long presented the boy
proudly at one of his famous "House Concerts."

When war came to Europe in 1914, the Brailowskys,
being of Russian birth, were interned. Influential friends
interceded for them and gained their release. They moved
to Switzerland, where Ferruccio Busoni, the distinguished
composer and pianist, was so impressed by Brailowsky's

playing that he adopted the boy as his protégé. From Switzerland, the family went on to Paris. There, in 1920, Brailowsky's début took place and proved so successful that engagements came to him thick and fast.

He played for Queen Elizabeth of Belgium who was so moved that she brought him to the attention of powerful friends. They, in turn, arranged for Brailowsky's first tour of South America. His initial concert there was attended sparsely, but word of his remarkable playing passed around so quickly that for his very next concert no tickets were available. Since then, no concert artist has drawn so well in South America as he. The price of tickets for his performance is frequently increased to $10, and even then they are so scarce that they are bought and sold in the black market. The South Americans never seem to get enough of him. On one tour he gave eleven concerts in Rio de Janeiro, six in Sao Paulo, six in Montevideo, three in Santiago—and at all times the halls were overcrowded. On another tour he gave seventeen concerts in two months at the Teatro Colon, and for each concert (despite the hall's seating capacity of 4,000) tickets were at a premium. His gross of $9,000 a concert is considered something of a record in South America.

After extensive tours of Europe and South America, Brailowsky came to this country, making his American début in New York on November 19, 1924. His playing so electrified both audience and critics that a tour originally scheduled for six weeks was extended to four months. After a hiatus of almost a dozen years, a period Brailowsky devoted to concert activity in Europe and South America, Brailowsky returned to America, making his reappearance on February 7, 1936. And from that time on he has played in this country extensively.

Up to the time of World War II, Brailowsky's home

was in Lausanne, Switzerland, overlooking Lake Geneva. He then established himself in this country where he now intends to maintain his permanent residence. When he travels on his tours he never consults travel agents, but plans all his own itineraries. He has made a hobby of memorizing timetables of all countries, knows when and where the leading trains of the world leave and arrive. He never goes anywhere without one of his pet dogs as a constant companion, and a doll, which he has come to look upon as a good-luck charm.

His many interests include: culturally—paintings, good conversation, languages, good books (his favorite single book is Tolstoy's *War and Peace* which he has read eight times); sports—tennis and motoring; relaxation—motion pictures (preferably gangster films). He is a rabid collector, preferably old clocks and household pets.

During World War II he was indefatigable in entertaining the Allied forces everywhere with his concerts. He was recently presented by the King of Denmark with the King Christian X Medal of Liberation for his "contribution to Denmark's cause during the years of the Nazi occupation."

6

RUDOLF SERKIN

◇◇

RUDOLF SERKIN has frequently been described as "the poet of the keyboard." Combining exquisite sensibilities, a classical intelligence, and an aristocratic style, he brings a deeply poetic instinct and a broad culture to the classic literature of the piano. He is master of detail: every effect is carefully planned, every nuance subtly prepared, every line fastidiously shaped and carved. Possessing magnificent digital control, and a consummate command of color, he draws from the keyboard exquisite sounds. The magnificent sweeps of Horowitz are not for him. He is more restrained and calculating. His playing is the personal and intimate musing of a deeply introspective artist.

He is the last word in modesty and self-effacement. An amusing story is told about his début in Vienna, which took place when he was twelve years old. His family decided to dress him à la Fauntleroy, with his hair elaborately curled. But after he had looked at himself in the hairdresser's mirror, he ran home and put his head under a faucet until all the curl came out!

The child grew into the man. Today, as then, Serkin refuses to let anything extraneous to his art enter into a concert performance. On the stage, he is modest, unpretentious, with an almost diffident kind of simplicity. He addresses himself directly to his music, and depends exclusively on that music to appeal to his public. At first glance, he may look (as one writer remarked) about as romantic as a grocery clerk. Tall and gangling, awkward and self-conscious in manner, he always seems ill at ease. His eyes appear to gaze half-startled through his spectacles. As he moves toward the piano, his gestures are abrupt, nervous. When he is seated there, his arms hang stiffly at his side; his head is slightly cocked. Yet the moment his fingers touch the keyboard he becomes magically touched with poetic glamour. A great spirit is speaking eloquent confidences, and, in the presence of such speech, the speaker suddenly becomes romanticized.

It is greatly to the credit of the American music public that it took to Serkin and placed him among its favorite pianists; the large audiences that acclaim him are testimony to the discriminating tastes of American music lovers. Horowitz and Artur Rubinstein inevitably arouse enthusiasm for their color and magnetism, their dazzling exhibition of pianistic virtuosity. But Serkin (like Artur Schnabel) has no stage appearance whatsoever. His gestures at the piano are rather clumsy, certainly not calculated to attract, and his playing is singularly undramatic. His appeal is exclusively a musical one; and his victory has been a musical one.

He was born in Eger, Czechoslovakia, on March 28, 1903. His father, formerly a singer in Russia, was led by the necessity of supporting a large family to abandon a musical career for business. He was a man of high ideals, and to him Rudolf owes his notably well-rounded development as a musician. Rudolf began playing the piano at the age of four, showing particular facility for sight-reading; by his fifth birthday, it was evident that he was a prodigy.

Father Serkin, however, had no intention of exploiting his son. "We do not want a prodigy," he said; "what we want is an artist." Though the Serkin family was in sad need of funds, the father refused consistently to consider concert enagements for the boy, insisting that Rudolf's boyhood be devoted to study.

An eminent Viennese musician, Alfred Grünfeld, heard Serkin when the boy was nine years old, and was so impressed by the performance that he arranged to have him come to Vienna. There he studied with Richard Robert. The fruits of this study became apparent when, in his twelfth year, he appeared as soloist with the Vienna Symphony Orchestra in the Mendelssohn G minor Concerto. The critics were lavish in their praise. A tempting concert tour was offered the boy, but it was summarily turned down. Instead, Rudolf continued with his studies, subsequently becoming a pupil of Arnold Schoenberg in composition.

The year of 1920 was a pivotal one for Serkin. His studies over, he planned to go to Paris. Post-war travel in Austria being difficult, Serkin discovered—when he arrived at the station too late to make his train—that another reservation for a Paris train would not be available for weeks. Disconsolate, he made his way back home. En route, he met a friend who invited him to a musical soirée that very evening. There he was introduced to the violinist Adolph Busch, thirteen years his senior, who had already made his mark in the music world. Busch and Serkin played several sonatas. When they finished, Busch told him: "You must come to Berlin and live with me. Next fall we will tour together."

In his mail the next morning, Serkin received a letter from Busch with the enclosure of a train ticket for Berlin. Thus Berlin, and not Paris, became Serkin's first important destination away from Vienna. He lived with the Busches, fondled four-year-old Irene Busch (who he little suspected would some day be his wife), and worked hard practicing with Adolf Busch. That fall, he made his Berlin début by performing the piano obbligato in Bach's Brandenburg Concerto No. 5, which was conducted by Busch. So boisterous was the acclaim accorded the young pianist, that an encore seemed in order. A little flustered, young Rudolf sat down at the piano and played the fifty-five minute *Goldberg Variations* of Bach!

He toured that season with Adolph Busch, and subsequently alone. In recitals, as guest of leading orchestras, in chamber-music performances with the Busch Quartet, in sonata recitals with Adolph Busch, Serkin showed sensitivity and refinement in his interpretation of the masterpieces of music. His sphere was the classic literature from Bach to Brahms, and in that sphere his was a uniquely eloquent voice.

In 1933, Serkin made his American début by appearing with Adolph Busch at the Coolidge Festival in Washington, D. C. A more official début took place on February 20, 1936 when he appeared as soloist with the New York Philharmonic-Symphony under Arturo Toscanini in two concertos by Mozart. At that performance it became evident that here was a high-minded, cultured and poetic musician. His American career thus handsomely launched by Toscanini, Serkin soon took a position of first importance among the pianists of our time.

Since then, Serkin has provided us with some of our most exciting aesthetic experiences. One recalls with peculiar nostalgic pleasure the three cycles of piano concertos which he undertook in New York with the National Orchestral Association. Beyond these, there are his recitals, his sonata concerts with Adolph Busch, his chamber-music concerts with the Busch Quartet and the Busch Chamber Orchestra—all bringing enrichment to our concert life season after season.

Serkin's long musical association with Adolph Busch became a more intimate bond in 1935 when he married Busch's daughter, Irene. Since then the Busches and the Serkins have lived either together or near each other. The Serkin household—a favorite rendezvous of musicians and the scene of continual music-making—is in Guilford, near Brattleboro, Vermont. There are four Serkin children: Ursula and Elizabeth were born in Switzerland in 1936 and 1939; John Arthur and Peter were born in this country in 1942 and 1947. All four are intensely musical. Rudolf Serkin does his practicing in a garage converted into a music studio. His extra-musical interests include skiing, mountain climbing, collecting tropical fish, and first editions of music.

7

MYRA HESS

◇◇

W HEN WAR broke out in Europe in September, 1939, Myra Hess was on the eve of embarking on her annual American tour. The British officials urged her not to cancel it, feeling that an artist like her, whose personal appeal in America was so great, and whose sensitive art had such a large following, could do yeomen service as a spokesman for Britain's cause. Other English artists were being sent to this country for a similar purpose: to create a stronger bond between the two English-speaking democracies during this critical period.

But Myra Hess could not be convinced that her duty as an Englishwoman rested in America. War-torn England, she knew, would need the solace and inspiration of great music, more than ever before. It would, of course, have been safer (and pleasanter) for an artist to concertize in the United States at this time, separated from suffering and death by three thousand miles of ocean. But Myra Hess was not thinking of personal safety. Gentle and soft-spoken, she can also, on occasion, reveal a strength of will that will not accept defeat. At moments of decision her eyes grow intense, the muscles of her face become taut. Thus must she have made what was probably the greatest decision of her life, and met it firmly: She would take an active part in her country's life-and-death struggle regardless of personal consequences. Doggedly, she went from one government bureau to the next, from one influential official to another, pulling wires, cajoling, begging, demanding that her American tour be permitted to be canceled. She wanted to fight for England in her own way.

And her own way was through music.

Eventually her perseverance won out, and she received official approval to remain in England. Before the first troops left England, she inaugurated a daily concert at noon in the cupola of the National Gallery in London. She had in mind a sort of sanctuary of great art in which the gruesome realities of modern warfare would not enter; a refuge for war-exhausted Londoners; a bombproof shelter for the human spirit.

At one of her first concerts she made her aim clear in a forthright and brief speech to her audience: "I want to keep this little oasis of peace going in the heart of London, and although we may be a small community, the principle of not being deterred by evil forces is important."

At first her concerts consisted solely of piano recitals. Then, as these noonday events began to attract capacity audiences who found them an escape, she expanded her programs to include other artists besides herself, in performances of an ambitious repertoire of chamber-music works. The great German masterpieces were not to be boycotted; on her programs Bach, Beethoven and Brahms appeared together with the English and French composers. For if Myra Hess was true to her native country, she was equally true to her artistic conscience.

When the air *blitzkrieg* descended on London in all its fury, it was regretfully thought by many Londoners that now the Hess concerts would come to their end. But this highly sensitive woman who in normal times could be reduced to tears at the sight of ugliness, would not give up. She arranged the construction of an underground shelter below the National Gallery to which she now transferred her concerts; that was her only concession to the dangers of the war. But to abandon London because it had now become a scene of danger never once entered her mind. Her work had to go on. Each day, punctually at eleven thirty in the morning, she could be seen making her way through the wreckage and havoc inflicted by the Nazi bombers of the preceding night, walking briskly from her home to the nearby National Gallery where she had an appointment with her fellow Londoners. And each day these victims of Hitler's barbarism, their nerves strained by the shattering air attack of the night before, their bodies exhausted by the work since dawn of putting out fires and clearing wreckage, their spirit depressed at the sight of the dead and the wounded, would make their way at noon to the underground auditorium of the National Gallery, there to hear the music of the ages. Sometimes it was so cold there that Myra Hess had to wear a fur coat while playing. Sometimes the destruction outside was so great that it seemed almost impossible to gain access to the underground auditorium. But the concerts went on, day by day, without interruption.

By the time the war came to an end there had taken place 1,698 concerts before a total audience estimated at a million. Approximately one thousand artists assisted Myra Hess in these performances. None of them accepted any compensation for their services; the small admission charge (approximately twenty cents) was used by Hess as a permanent fund with which to assist those musicians in England impoverished by the war. Never once during the entire war was a single scheduled performance canceled "Taxi drivers learned to love Mozart," Myra Hess revealed proudly, "and cooks and waiters became friends with Beethoven's chamber music."

It is, of course, not possible to measure the extent to which these concerts contributed to the high morale of Londoners in the darkest hours of the war. But the size of audiences that crowded the Myra Hess concerts every day suggests that the role these concerts played in the war effort was by no means negligible. When, in 1936, King George V conferred on Myra Hess the appointment of Commander of the Order of the British Empire (his last official act) he did so because of her indisputable position in English music. But when, in June 1941, King George VI bestowed on her the highest honor which can be given to a woman, that of Dame Commander of the British Empire, it was because she also joined the ranks of England's heroes.

When, the war over, Myra Hess returned to the American concert scene after an absence of more than seven years—at Town Hall, New York, on October 12, 1946—the capacity audience rose to its feet to welcome her, a spontaneous expression of homage not only to a very great artist, but also to a very great woman.

Myra Hess' position as the world's foremost woman pianist has long been secure. Like Serkin's, hers is a poetic temperament which expresses itself in sensitivity of touch, delicacy of phrasing, and a singing tone of many colors. Her interpretations of the classic literature are scholarly and marked by an ever-fresh approach. Her extraordinary technique is disciplined and is servant to the thought and mood she is trying to project.

She was born in Hampstead, near London, on February 25, 1890, and began the study of the piano when she was five years old. At seven, she passed the entrance examinations for Trinity College, London. Subsequent music study took place at the Royal Academy in London (under a scholarship) where her teacher was Tobias Matthay.

After a long and careful period of preparation, Myra Hess made her début in London in 1907. She created a fine impression and was forthwith engaged to appear as soloist with the London Philharmonic Orchestra, directed by Sir Thomas Beecham, in Beethoven's Concerto in G major. This performance established her reputation in England. She then undertook an extensive European tour.

Not until her recognition was widespread in Europe did she essay her first visit to this country. On January 17, 1922, she appeared in this country for the first time. W. J. Henderson wrote: "Myra Hess is not merely a great woman pianist; she is a great pianist without limitation. She has a fine and strong mind, capable of long perspectives and deep penetration and trained thoroughly in musicianship. She has imagination, which is the vital necessity of all art. . . . She has the tone and the technical facility to carry out perfectly her artistic intentions." Henderson was articulating what the audience felt about her, and has felt about her ever since.

Fritz Kreisler

III

VIOLINISTS

❖◇◇◇❖

1. *Fritz Kreisler*
2. *Jascha Heifetz*
3. *Yehudi Menuhin*
4. *Nathan Milstein*
5. *Joseph Szigeti*

1

FRITZ KREISLER

◇◇◇

Fate Being what it is, it is not beyond the realm of possibility that the name of Fritz Kreisler will descend to posterity for a reason other than that he has been one of the greatest violinists of our age. One can almost foresee some musical dictionary of the 21st century referring to Kreisler in this fashion: "He was one of the most distinguished artists of his generation, and a composer of many delightful morsels for his instrument. He is remembered today only because of a hoax which he perpetrated on the entire musical world of his time, presenting his own compositions as products of such masters as Vivaldi, Martini, Couperin, Pugnani, Francoeur, etc. For more than thirty years, this hoax went undetected, until the composer himself revealed the truth."

Present-day music lovers will surely recall that about a decade ago the world was startled to learn that those violin gems which Kreisler had for so many years been featuring as the works of masters were, in reality, original with him. Yet, as Kreisler himself confessed to his close friends, he had had no intention of "pulling the nose" of the music world. When he first presented these pieces he explained laboriously that he had stumbled across the original manuscripts in European monasteries and had freely adapted them for the violin. He did this not to test the critical acumen of his fellow musicians, but merely as a temporary, though ethically questionable, expedient of a young and unknown violinist who wished to have his own works performed more widely. However, with the deception far more successful than Kreisler ever dared to hope, he discovered that it was not quite so easy to confess to the world that he had quietly palmed off a fraud. He therefore nursed his secret, always alert for some propitious moment in which to relieve himself of it gracefully.

The moment arrived when the distinguished New York music critic, Olin Downes, attempted to trace the source of "Pugnani's *Praeludium and Allegro*." He communicated first with Kreisler's publishers, and then with Kreisler himself. He was told unequivocally, and without the slightest attempt at subterfuge on the part of the violinist, that the piece was original; that, as a matter of fact, most of the other so-called Kreisler "transcriptions," too, were original. And one could almost hear a sigh of infinite relief accompanying the confession.

It was to be expected that musicians and critics should greet the hoax as if it were a personal offense, with grumbles of anger and denunciations of Kreisler's "artistic dishonesty." A scattered few met the confession with what Kreisler described as "good humor and splendid sportsmanship," but, for the most part, Kreisler was treated with scathing criticism. "We wish to apply the term discreditable to the whole transaction from start to finish," commented one eminent music journal editorially. Some critics, headed by Ernest Newman, flayed Kreisler with merciless lashes of their verbal whips. The music world felt somewhat silly and not a little awkward and embarrassed to learn that it had been a victim of a fraud for which all of musical history can find no counterpart. There have been

composers who have concealed their identities under man-
ufactured pseudonyms, but never before this had a composer masqueraded his music behind the great names of
the past, to have the music accepted as genuine without
question or suspicion. "It is as though Mr. Keats published
poems under the name of Herrick or Spenser," pointed
out Ernest Newman.

Yet studying the entire affair in retrospect, musicians
should not have been taken altogether by surprise. More
than twenty years ago, Kreisler presented his *Liebesfreud,
Liebesleid,* and *Schön Rosmarin* as "transcriptions" of
posthumous pieces by Josef Lanner. It was only because a
Viennese critic assailed Kreisler for his impudence in including his own *Caprice Viennois* in the same group with
"these gems of Lanner" that Kreisler indignantly confessed
that these pieces were actually his own and not Lanner's.
This episode might have passed without much publicity
at the time, but musicians were well acquainted with it
and often referred to it. One would therefore have expected that Kreisler's other transcriptions would be more
rigorously scrutinized, particularly since a warning was
flashed on the titlepage of every Kreisler publication:
"The original manuscripts used for these transcriptions
are the private property of Mr. Fritz Kreisler and are now
published for the first time; they are, moreover, so freely
treated that *they constitute, in fact, original works."* The
italics are mine; but they might easily have been Kreisler's.

Perhaps some musicians suspected the authenticity of
this music. It may have been only because the fraud was
much too perfect that the world permitted itself to be
duped for so long a time.

It is very doubtful, however, that Kreisler's confession
has diminished his enormous stature to a perceptible degree in the eyes of his audience. Few artists of our time—

with the possible exception of Toscanini—have inspired such adoration from audiences throughout the world as Kreisler has since 1900. An adoration such as this is not so easily dissipated. Even when the incident was fresh in the minds of the music public, the feeling was strong among many that the deception was, after all, nothing worse than a youthful indiscretion, and that Kreisler later handled with fearless honesty the very difficult situation of making an open confession. And the unquestionable skill with which he had mimicked the styles of the old masters could not fail to elicit a certain measure of well-deserved admiration.

In any case, Kreisler's singular fascination for his audience was in no great danger. With the first unpleasantness and bitterness forgotten, the incident even brought him additional glory.

The enormous attraction that Kreisler holds for his audience arises not merely from the magic of violin and bow, but also from his unique personal charm. The poise and refinement of his platform manner, the dignity and yet cordial warmth of his relationship with his audience, have an appeal the strength of which cannot be questioned. His soft smile, in response to an ovation, is of ineffable sweetness, and his eyes are warm and kind. He possesses, to an unusual degree, the ability to create at his concerts an intimacy and personal contact between himself and his audience which succeed in making even the largest concert hall assume the friendliness of a small drawing-room.

For a long time now, Kreisler's personality has been touched with glamour in the eyes of his audience. His intense humanity and great heart have probably inspired as much admiration as his sublime playing; his activities during and after the First World War, for example. It need not be retold in detail that he sent a large proportion of his earnings to Austria to help alleviate the terrible suffering and despair of his fellow countrymen during the postwar period. It is said that Mrs. Kreisler personally interested herself in the future of forty-two orphans, because she had promised their dying fathers in the hospital to look after them. And Kreisler was directly responsible for the support of some fifteen hundred starving artists. For a period of more than five years, all his earnings flowed into Austria, where his wife contributed her marvelous energy in dividing the money among the sick, the starving, and the crushed. His devotion to charitable work during these years was so great that everything else pertaining to his art and life assumed secondary importance.

Ernö Balogh, who, for a short time, was Kreisler's accompanist, told me an anecdote that is particularly illuminating in giving us insight into a great character. Shortly after the war, while concertizing in Norway, Kreisler was invited to have tea with the King—an honor which most artists would have accepted with unmitigated delight. Kreisler, however, apologized for not coming, explaining that he was too busy. That afternoon he remained in his hotel to do secretarial work for a series of charities which he was conducting for needy Europeans. "But," Balogh said to him with surprise, "you told His Majesty that you were too busy to have tea with him, and now you are doing only charity work!" "Charity work—that is something else," Kreisler answered softly. "Why should I go out of my way to have tea with a king? With a great thinker or humanitarian—yes, I would gladly spend precious time with such a man. But a king? No, thank you. It's much more important to spend the time in helping these poor starving people!"

"And that," added Balogh as a commentary, "is a characteristic Kreisler gesture."

Such human generosity could not, of course, fail to make Kreisler a singularly appealing figure. Equally important in inspiring the admiration of his public is his wit, spontaneous and pointed, which has frequently been quoted and repeated in music circles. One story is well known: At one time a Chicago heiress invited him to play at a private party she was giving, and inquired his fee. "Three thousand dollars," Kreisler told her. "The fee, Mr. Kreisler, is satisfactory. But, of course, you realize that you are not to mingle with the guests." "In that case," answered Kreisler, "the fee is only two thousand."

What has aroused most adulation among music audiences is Kreisler's broad cultural background, unique among musicians. His many talents, which branch out into so many diverse directions, have long been subjects for discussion and awe among concert goers.

He is almost as gifted with piano as with the violin; and now it is more apparent than ever before that his creative talent is not much less significant than his interpretative. He can paint with a sure and tasteful brush. Early in his life he studied in the famous atelier of Julien in Paris, where he revealed such great promise that it seemed that art and not music would become his life work. He is well schooled in mathematics and the sciences, and has a very intimate acquaintance with medicine. His linguistic talents are enormous. Not merely is he able to speak eight languages with fluency, with a solid foundation of Greek and Latin, but he is also a devoted student of philology. He is a lover of books—a famous collector, as a matter of fact; and he has an admirable literary background. His fine critical sense is the result of an intellectual background that embraces philosophy, logic and metaphysics.

Obviously, he has been fed on a well-balanced cultural diet, and his appetite is so keen that he has been able to take more than a mere superficial taste of each dish. The consequence is a fertile background of scholarship. It is this enormous culture that is reflected in his violin-playing and that gives it a great part of its individuality and character. With age, Kreisler's technique may falter and his tone may become diluted; but his phrasing, his dynamics, his deftly superimposed nuances—fruits of maturity and wisdom—are unmistakably fingerprinted on his performances.

Almost any violinist—not excluding even Heifetz or Menuhin—will sound like any other half-dozen great violinists in playing certain small pieces. Kreisler, however, is unable to play twelve bars of music without disclosing himself. In this connection, I am reminded of a story which Kreisler likes to tell, and which is indicative of the way in which the entire world is familiar with his style.

Kreisler was browsing in an antique shop in Antwerp when he came upon a cheap violin. He called the pawnbroker to him—"an old Jew who seemed to have stepped out of a picture by Rembrandt," as Kreisler himself described him—and asked the price. Then, somewhat playfully, he took his own violin out of the case and asked the old Jew if he would care to purchase it. The old Jew looked at the violin, handled it with careful fingers, and then said: "I am afraid I am not rich enough to pay you what this violin is worth." Then, as an afterthought, he added: "Would you please wait here two minutes? I'll dash home and bring you an Amati violin which will certainly interest you." In a few minutes he returned—with a policeman. "That man," the Jew cried, pointing a finger at the somewhat bewildered violinist, "is a thief. Arrest him! He has in his possession a violin belonging to Fritz Kreisler!"

In vain did Kreisler protest that he himself was the great

violinist; the fact that he had left his passport in his hotel room did not simplify the situation. Finally, Kreisler put the violin under his chin and played *Schön Rosmarin.* "There's no doubt about it," the pawnbroker said with a voice that cracked with bewilderment. "This gentleman simply *can't* be anyone else than Fritz Kreisler!"

What distinguishes Kreisler's playing from that of so many other violinists is not merely a profound culture which brings new significance to every phrase or accent. Nor does it lie in technique. A dissection of his playing might focus attention on the warmth and humanity of his tone, the resilience of his bow in *spiccato* passages, or the incomparable grace of his trill; but these are not enough to explain the true nature of his art. What does explain it is rather an indefinable quality sometimes vaguely called the "Kreisler charm." To explain Kreisler's violin-playing precisely, one must borrow the term that has long been applied to the city of Kreisler's birth, Vienna—*Gemütlichkeit.* Kreisler's violin-playing is essentially Viennese in its grace, fullness of heart, zest for life. It is the embodiment of the Viennese spirit of the Schubert *Ländler,* the waltzes of Lanner and Johann Strauss, the operettas of Franz Lehár. His art is Viennese in its subtle refinement and in the intriguing sparkle of personality.

For two centuries the Viennese people have had a felicitous word with which to describe life in the Austrian capital. That word, *flott*—implying zest and buoyancy—might most aptly describe the violin-playing of Fritz Kreisler.

Legend would have us believe that Kreisler was driven by an uncontrollable force to music and the violin from his earliest years. The truth, however, is that as a child Kreisler detested the playing of the violin and that, throughout his entire career, he periodically attempted to escape from his instrument.

He was born in Vienna on February 2, 1875, and was given his first lessons on the violin by his father, an eminent Viennese physician and ichthyologist. It was only with the greatest difficulty that his father could induce the boy to practice his exercises; he persisted only because Fritz disclosed such extraordinary talent from the very first. At the age of seven, Fritz Kreisler made his public début, playing several small pieces on the violin on a program featuring Carlotta Patti (sister of the immortal Adelina). His taste and musicianship were both evident, and it was decided to enroll him in the Vienna Conservatory for an intensive course of music study. Despite the fact that the minimum age for entering the Conservatory was fourteen, Fritz, aged seven, was immediately admitted. After three years of study under Joseph Hellmesberger (one of the most famous Viennese musicians of the time, and in a sense the city's musical arbiter), Kreisler received the gold medal for violin-playing. During these years his musical taste was permanently shaped by performances he heard given by Joseph Joachim and Anton Rubinstein—performances that he has never forgotten.

From Vienna he went to Paris, where he was admitted to the Paris Conservatory, as a pupil of Massart in violin-playing and of Delibes in theory. Once again he astounded his professors, this time by winning the *Premier Grand Prix* for violin-playing in his twelfth year, in a competition in which every other entrant was some ten years his senior. However, the practicing of exercises was, as he confesses today, always an ordeal for him; it was only with the greatest reluctance that he would pick up violin and bow for his daily study. Even many years later, at the height of his career, he reduced his practicing to a minimum, far below the number of hours that other violinists require to keep their fingers agile.

It is incorrect to believe that Kreisler's artistic path has been one of glory from the first. When, in 1888, he came to America on his first concert tour in a series of joint recitals with Moriz Rosenthal, the pianist (Kreisler was then only fourteen), he played charmingly enough to receive a few kind notices from the critics; but to call his American début sensational would be to stretch the truth to the point of exaggeration. As a matter of fact, his talent was so tepidly accepted that, when he returned to Vienna shortly thereafter, he was found unsuitable even for a position as second violinist in the Vienna Philharmonic Orchestra.

This mild reception as a violinist convinced his father that the boy's future lay in directions other than music; and so the violin was put aside—permanently, it was then believed. Fritz was enrolled in the Vienna Gymnasium to prepare for the career of medicine. For several years he conformed to the strict discipline of student life, and revealed an astonishing adaptability to his studies. Then, somewhat impatient with the routine, he suddenly decided to return to art. The violin he still avoided; this time he felt called to painting, not to music. He left for Paris, worked hard there, and received the glowing praises of Julien. He then went to Rome for further study. Finally, the lure of art having palled just as he was about to achieve success, Fritz returned to Vienna to prepare for a stiff army examination. He passed with high honors, and for a full year wore the uniform of an officer in the regiment of Uhlans.

Soldiering, however, could never appeal permanently to a person of Kreisler's keen intellect. So he abandoned it—once again with success awaiting him in his newly chosen profession. Since no other career was open to him, he returned—not a little reluctantly, he confesses—to the violin.

His former suppleness of fingers gone, Kreisler decided to retire to the country for eight weeks of indefatigable practicing. He worked assiduously, pouring his entire devotion, energy, and application into his technique; and he emerged from this eight-week period of retirement and study the greatest violinist of his generation.

Kreisler made his return début in Berlin in 1899, but several years passed before his concerts received anything beyond an apathetic response. "I was as great a fiddler then as I have ever been since," Kreisler informs us; but his playing failed to inflame the imagination of his public. Avoiding the shallow and the sensational, placing less emphasis upon pyrotechnics and more upon musical content, his performances were too serious for immediate recognition.

However, when his full stature eventually became obvious—particularly with his grandiose conception of the Bach solo sonatas for violin, and the violin concertos of Bach, Beethoven, and Brahms—it was America that was one of the first countries to give him full recognition. After several tours through this country, from 1901 to 1903, which were nothing short of sensational, his supreme position among the violinists of his day could no longer be questioned.

While en route to America in 1902, Fritz Kreisler met aboard ship a charming American woman, Harriet Lies. Their friendship developed rapidly. In November of that year they were married. Theirs was a marriage of true minds, which has offered no little inspiration and strength to the great violinist.

When war broke out in Europe in 1914, Kreisler was vacationing in Switzerland. Without hesitating for a moment—Viennese blood is hot blood!—he returned to his country to rejoin his former regiment in Galicia. All the gruesome privations of a soldier's life were now the fate of the world's greatest violinist. "For two days I went without taking off my clothes," Kreisler himself wrote of his weeks in the trenches,* "sleeping on wet grass, or in the mud, or in the swamps. One night, while sleeping, we were drenched to the skin by torrential rains. . . . We were looking like shaggy wolves from the necessity of subsisting on next to nothing. I remember having gone for more than three days at a time without any food whatsoever, and many a time we had to lick the dew from the grass for want of water."

On September 6, 1914, an unexpected cavalry attack from the Russians descended upon Lemberg, and Kreisler was a victim. A lance pierced his foot. With the help of an orderly, he made his way safely to the hospital.

Discharged from the army with high honors, Kreisler felt that there was only one avenue left through which he could help his country. He undertook an extensive concert tour through America that would have sapped the energy and exhausted the strength of a physique stronger than his; but he could do it bravely and cheerfully because he knew that his bulging income would bring relief to his crushed compatriots.

With America's entry into World War I, Kreisler's position in this country became embarrassing. He had been a soldier in the enemy's camp. He had openly confessed that his earnings from concerts were sent to Austria to relieve suffering. He was too honest to renounce his allegiance to

* *Four Weeks in the Trenches,* by Fritz Kreisler. Houghton Mifflin Company, 1915.

the country of his birth simply because of expediency. As a result, abuse, insult, and hatred fell upon him from pulpit and press, from clubs and patriotic societies. Only one move was possible: he announced his retirement from concert work, and isolated himself in Maine where, in a deserted corner, he found consolation in his violin, in gardening, and in playing chess.

In the winter of 1919, Fritz Kreisler once again emerged from retirement to appear on the concert platform. The concert in which he first made his reappearance will never be forgotten by those of us who were present. When he came on the stage of Carnegie Hall in New York, the entire audience—now recovering from its former war hysteria —rose spontaneously to welcome him. For more than five minutes it remained on its feet in honor of a great artist and a still greater personality.

And it has remained on its feet ever since.

His seventieth birthday behind him, Kreisler cannot be said to have defied time in his art. His technique is no longer as sure as it once was; his intonation is no longer precise; his tone is less pure. But those who hear him today are still conscious of a great master speaking out of the fullness of a great heart and out of the inexhaustible storehouse of a noble spirit.

For a while, in 1941, it looked as though his magnificent career had been brought to a sudden and tragic close. One day when, absorbed in thought, he was crossing a New York avenue at 42nd Street, a truck hit him, causing a fracture of the skull, as well as other internal injuries. For days he lay in a coma, and it was feared that the accident had affected him mentally as well as physically. In any event, it seemed probable that even if he recovered physically—in itself a miracle—his days as a concert artist were permanently over.

Actually, his body responded to treatment and, after several weeks, was on its way to recovery. But would he be able to play again? One day, his wife brought him his violin and, as a test, begged him to play for her a passage from the Mendelssohn Concerto. Falteringly, the invalid brought violin to chin, and bow to strings. There was a moment's hesitation—a moment that must have been an eternity to Mrs. Kreisler. Then the tone came full and clear, and the beautiful Mendelssohn melody soared as if on wings. Kreisler was still the master. . . .

Jascha Heifetz

2

JASCHA HEIFETZ

◇◇

THE WORD "Heifetz" does not appear in the English dictionary, but one sometimes wonders whether it does not deserve a permanent place there. For musicians and laymen alike, "Heifetz" has become an eloquent word descriptive of the *ne plus ultra* of violin virtuosity. Mothers who raise their children to be prodigies speak of them as "little Heifetzes." Critics employing their most precious superlative on a violinist will write: "He plays like a Heifetz."

Glorification came to Heifetz long ago. His artistic career began sensationally when he was six years old ("What were you before that?" once asked the irrepressible Harpo Marx of Heifetz. "Just a bum?") and has continued ever since to amass layer upon layer of triumph. In his thirty and more years of active concertizing, Heifetz has traveled almost a million and a half miles. He has played in every corner of the world, and everywhere he is equally admired. He concertized during the days of the great Russian upheaval after the 1917 revolution, during the Sinn Fein uprisings in Ireland, during the 1923 earthquake in Japan, and in the midst of Gandhi-troubled Bombay. At the Lewisohn Stadium in New York he performed before one of the largest single audiences to attend a concert there.

He is known wherever music is made. Even to those who rarely enter a concert hall, the name of Jascha Heifetz has an aura of magic.

To music lovers, of course, Heifetz has legendary fame. Violinists will tell you that he is the greatest technician of the violin alive; in no other's playing can be found the cleanness and despatch with which Heifetz performs even the most uncompromisingly difficult passages. But lovers of great music have long ago learned that he is not merely the perfect instrumental mechanic. He performs with incomparable insight, with a beautiful sense of style, perfect phrasing, and, above all else, an ability to convey the inmost message of the composer—whether in works like the great concertos of Beethoven, Brahms, and Mendelssohn, the fireworks of Vieuxtemps and Wieniawski, the romantic effusions of Glazunov and Tchaikovsky, or such modern masterpieces as the concertos of Elgar, Sibelius, and Prokofiev. That his lightning fingers are infallible has been widely publicized; but with this goes a really profound musicianship and taste, together with insight and discernment. There will be few to deny, I am sure, that he stands with the immortal interpreters of all time.

Heifetz has been fed on fame and adulation from earliest childhood. Born in Vilna in 1901—on February 2, which is also Kreisler's birthday—he was the son of Ruvin Heifetz, violinist in a Vilna theater orchestra. Very early he showed himself extremely sensitive to music: when he was only eight months old his face would shine when his father played a beautiful melody on the violin; but when a dissonance was sounded, the infant's face would reflect actual pain. After a time these reactions to sound became so marked that, almost playfully, Ruvin Heifetz bought his son a quarter-size violin for his third birthday. What had been intended as a mere toy for a child was soon to become an instrument for serious musical expression. Jascha was given a few elementary lessons by his father, learning with such eagerness that he was soon given a systematic course of study.

When Jascha reached his fifth birthday, his talent was so evident that his father felt the responsibility of training a genius too formidable for his own capabilities. He entered Jascha in the Royal School of Music at Vilna, placing him under the instruction of Elias Malkin. One year later, the child was ready for his first concert appearance. In Kovno, he played the Mendelssohn violin concerto with an aplomb and self-assurance that amazed the audience of a thousand. His tone, though small, was firm and round. His little fingers coped with the technical difficulties of the last movement with bewildering precision. For the following two years the child was scheduled to give periodic public performances in Russia. Everywhere he was spoken of as the *wunderkind* without equal, a phenomenon of nature, a human miracle, so to speak.

It was as a wonder-boy that he made his never-to-be-forgotten American début at Carnegie Hall on October 27, 1917, and it was as a wonder-boy that he then achieved a triumph that only a handful of concert artists of our generation have equaled. Music lovers in the audience were overwhelmed by the exhibition; critics sang paeans of praise; and violinists were dumbfounded. A famous anecdote has it that Leopold Godowsky, the pianist, and Mischa Elman, the violinist, were seated in a box at the concert. During the intermission, Elman made what he thought was an innocent remark. "Terribly hot, isn't it?" he asked Godowsky. "Not for pianists," was Godowsky's annihilating retort.

In the spring of 1934 Heifetz was given a rousing welcome when, after seventeen years of absence, he returned to his native country for a series of concerts. Musicians came from as far as Siberia for his first concert. People sold clothing and furniture to obtain the price of admission for one of his performances. Crowds stood on the streets outside the concert hall, shouting their praise. "That," Heifetz has said, "was the greatest emotional experience of my life."

When Heifetz was eight years old, he came into contact with the person who was probably the greatest single influence in his career. Leopold Auer, professor of the violin at the St. Petersburg Conservatory of Music, came to Vilna on a concert tour. Malkin, a personal friend of Auer, talked enthusiastically about his prodigy pupil: Jascha had technique and taste comparable to those of a fully mature artist. But Auer was impatient with Malkin's rhapsodies. He had heard *wunderkinder* to a point of satiation; they all bored him. Moreover, at the moment, he was too busy, and physically too fatigued, to listen to a prodigy. Another time, perhaps . . . but Malkin would not recognize defeat. He begged, then insisted, that Auer hear for himself. Finally, Auer relented. Little Jascha, accompanied by his father, appeared before the master and, with little ceremony, placed fiddle under chin and despatched the Mendelssohn concerto and the twenty-fourth caprice of Paganini. And Auer—who had protested his impatience with prodigies—embraced the boy and told him that he had not heard such a performance in a long time. He urged Jascha to come to St. Petersburg to become his pupil at the Conservatory.

Father Heifetz sold his belongings, resigned his position at the theater, and took his boy to St. Petersburg. At first, there were disheartening disappointments and obstacles for the Heifetz family. When they came to call on Auer, the professor did not recognize Jascha and, thinking him just another "prodigy," refused to open his door to him. When finally he identified Jascha as the Vilna wonder child, the period for entrance into the Conservatory had passed, and Auer's class was filled to capacity. But he used his influence and Heifetz was permitted to enter the class of Auer's assistant for one term. But—even with these difficulties surmounted—the path did not stretch clear for him. Jews were not then allowed permanent residence in St. Petersburg. Though exception was made for Conservatory students, none was made for their families. For a while it seemed that Ruvin Heifetz would have to return to Vilna, leaving Jascha alone in St. Petersburg. But the Conservatory director presently found a solution: he entered father Heifetz, aged 40, as a pupil at the Conservatory!

The way now cleared, young Heifetz proceeded to perfect himself as a violinist. After his first six months at the Conservatory, he became a pupil of Auer, and his progress from that time on was so rapid as to amaze even a callous professor. Auer freely confessed that he had never had a pupil such as this, who seemed able to do everything with the violin, and always in good taste.

The admirable American violinist, Albert Spalding, was once invited by the pedagogue Leopold Auer to come to a class as a visitor and hear a promising pupil. In his charming autobiography * Mr. Spalding has described what happened:

"A small boy stood up to play. He had only recently graduated to a full-sized violin, and it made him look even smaller than he was. One of Fra Angelico's seraphs seemed to have stepped from his background of goldleaf, disguised himself in modern dress, and exchanged a trumpet for a fiddle. He

* *Rise to Follow,* by Albert Spalding. Henry Holt & Co., 1943.

played the Ernst concerto. It is not one of my favorites; its unsubstantial themes might have had a naïve charm if treated simply, but faithful to the tradition of the day they were a continuous scenic railway of coasting thirds and ascending octaves, the work being designed to amaze rather than to please. Needless to say, its technical difficulties tax the most seasoned veteran. What a cruel test, I thought, for a child!

But I quickly found that there was no need for apprehension. The first flourish of fingered octaves was attacked with a kind of nonchalant aplomb; the tone was firm, flowing, and edgeless, the intonation of fleckless purity. A kind of inner grace made itself felt in the shaping of the phrase. I completely forgot the tawdriness of the piece in the elegance and distinction of its delivery. I had never heard such perfect technique from a child.

Jascha, they called him—Jascha Heifetz.

While the boy was playing, Auer strode nervously about the room, glancing at me now and then to appraise my reactions. His dark, restless eyes danced with delight as the wonder boy threaded his effortless way through the tortuous technical problems. He expected nothing less than paralyzed astonishment from me—nor was he disappointed. He would turn away with a helpless shrug of the shoulders as if to say: 'Was there ever anything like it?' Other talented students performed later, but they were eclipsed by this miniature wizard in his early teens."

During this period of study with Auer, concert work was not abandoned. The boy's fame spread throughout Europe. He played at the International Exposition in Odessa, where he was so idolized that a police guard was necessary to protect him from the admiring masses. He gave a concert in St. Petersburg which evoked thunderous acclaim. There were appearances in Austria and Germany, as well. Whenever he played, critics said that Heifetz, the boy, was already a full-grown artist, and among the great-

est. When in 1914 he performed at the Berlin Philharmonic concerts, its conductor, the incomparable Artur
Nikisch, admitted that he had never before heard such
violin playing.

Two years later, in the company of Professor Auer,
Heifetz went to Christiana (now Oslo), where once again
he became a public idol, performing before royalty, pampered and petted wherever he went. His travels continued
—to Japan by way of Siberia, and then to the United States.

On October 27, 1917, the wonder-boy of the violin gave
his first American concert at Carnegie Hall. His program
included the *Chaconne* of Vitali, the D minor concerto of
Wieniawski, the twenty-fourth caprice of Paganini, and
morsels (such as the Schubert-Wilhelmj *Ave Maria,* and
the Beethoven-Auer *March* from *The Ruins of Athens*)
which have since become inextricably associated with his
name.

How triumphant his début was can be most accurately
gauged by the ecstasy of the music critics. They had witnessed a phenomenon that startled and electrified them.
They did not mince words. "He is a modern miracle,"
wrote Pitts Sanborn. "He is a perfect violinist," reported
Sigmund Spaeth. "He rose above his instrument and the
music written for it," commented H. E. Krehbiel. "This
modern young Orpheus seems to do all the things with a
violin which a fabled charmer accomplished with a lyre,"
wrote Leonard Liebling; "he remains unapproached in
the perfection of his finger and bow manipulation, the refined wistfulness of his tone, and the unique appeal of his
apparently impersonal relation to his playing." And Herbert F. Peyser: "The newcomer plays with a tone so lustrous and silken, so fragrant, so intoxicatingly sweet, that
only the molten gold of Fritz Kreisler can be conjured up
in comparison. But though it wrings the tears from the

eyes by its lambent beauty, its vibrancy and infinite play of magical color, its nature bespeaks a singular aristocratic purity rather than an unrelieved sensuousness, though its power of emotional conveyance and suggestion is unparalleled."

For the next few years, the stature of Heifetz dominated the concert world. He concertized more extensively than any other living violinist, and his following everywhere was fabulous. His box-office earnings were unparalleled. He was the magician of the violin, and his audience came to be enchanted.

But, as the years passed, a certain dissatisfaction with Heifetz's playing arose. He was the perfect mechanic, true —the consummate technical master of his instrument, but music was much more than technique or mechanics. Where were the pulse, the heartbeat, the warm blood of the concertos of Mendelssohn and Brahms, the deep emotion in the Beethoven concerto, when Heifetz played them? Where, in his music, was there that dissecting analysis, that insight and understanding which one should expect from the playing of a great artist? Some called Heifetz cold, impersonal, too objective. The music he performed, they said, was as cold as a slab of marble—beautifully sculptured but lacking the essential vibrancy of a living organism.

The truth was—though it could hardly be recognized at the time—that Heifetz was undergoing a transition as an artist. He was reacting more and more strongly against the Russian sensuousness, the outpouring of sentiment, the emotional extravagances which were part and parcel of his Auer training. And, in reacting strongly, he had gone to the opposite extreme. Besides, this was a period of difficult emotional adjustment for Heifetz, and his art inevitably suffered.

But when this transition period was over Heifetz emerged a far greater artist than he had been before. He was still the wonder boy of 1917, still the incomparable technician. But, more important, there was now discovered in his playing a richer vein, a deeper but more controlled emotionalism, wisdom, mellowness. He no longer "despatched" the great sonatas and concertos of the masters. They were now reborn and revitalized under his fingers—as all great music is when it passes through the hands of a great and sensitive artist.

In his youth, his thick crop of hair clustered over his brow, his long, lean face and slight build were his identifying trademarks as an artist. Today, little in his appearance conforms to the traditional conception of the musician. His hair is clipped short and combed back neatly. His face has assumed a roundness of contour. The nose descends sharply from a high forehead and from between eyes of inexpressible sadness to overlook lips that are thin and sensitive. His physique is muscular and resilient, revealing the discipline which comes from a life devoted to boating, swimming, ball-playing, wood-chopping. His dress is always meticulously correct, whether he is indulging in outdoor sport or is entertaining guests in his living room. Indeed, his extensive wardrobe has long been the object of gentle ridicule among his artist friends.

In 1928, Heifetz married the beautiful Florence Vidor of Hollywood; two children were born to them, Josepha and Robert. Twenty years later, Heifetz was married a second time, to Frances Spiegelberg. The keynotes of his home in Beverly Hills are simplicity and good taste. There is no excess ornamentation, no ostentatious display of wealth. The furniture has dignity as well as comfort. Books, music, phonograph records, original paintings set the tone of culture. To a large degree, the comfortable unpretentiousness of this home reflects the nature of its owners. The Heifetzes are essentially simple people who enjoy the open country more than they do the febrile city. The hills offer Heifetz himself far greater satisfaction than night clubs. Hikes or gardening appeal to him more than cocktail parties, even though he does derive a measure of enjoyment from giving parties and drinking in moderation. Everything he does, he does in moderation and with a healthy balance. He has little use for excesses of any kind.

When he gives a party it is usually a musicale—an intimate concert of chamber music in which Heifetz joins with other distinguished musicians. This, his greatest pleasure, opens to him a world of music distinct from that which is his as a virtuoso. Away from music, Heifetz likes good literature (he reads voraciously, and is a collector of books—once, of rare editions), and great paintings (he is a friend of Diego Rivera and a sponsor of Gregory Gluckmann).

The simpler pleasures complete a full life: ping-pong, which he plays extraordinarily well; long walks; photography; gardening, in which he indulges zestfully, with no effort to spare his precious hands. Sometimes, when a temporary depression of spirit sets in, he finds relaxation and escape in a long drive through country roads. In his driving, as in almost everything else he does, he is more than passably adept.

Of his possessions, he is proudest of his precious collection of violins which not only includes a treasurable Stradivarius (1731) and Guarnerius (1742) but various unusual items. One of his violins is made of 2,750 matches glued together; another is contained within the knob of a walking stick; a third is made entirely of aluminum. "I'm particularly partial to that aluminum violin," Heifetz once remarked. "When anything goes wrong with it I can send it to a plumber." The most sentimental item in this collection is a quarter-size instrument in a homemade case— Heifetz's first violin. He received it as a gift from his uncle Naoum when he returned to concertize in Russia in 1934.

In his music, he has the seriousness of purpose, the integrity, the wholesome honesty of the true artist. His career has been untouched by any opportunism, cheapness, or debasement of the high artistic standards he has set for himself. Few artists of our time have been as true to themselves and to their profession as Heifetz. His first adventure in making motion pictures is a case in point. He went to make a picture for Samuel Goldwyn only after he had become convinced that the screen was now capable of excellent musical reproduction; tempting offers had come to him from Hollywood long before he accepted this one. The film he finally made, *They Shall Have Music,* was voted by the educators of this country as the greatest single contribution made to music appreciation by the motion-picture industry.

Characteristic, too, was his first appearance for G.I.'s during World War II when he enlisted himself and his art to the war effort. This took place at Camp Roberts in California. After tuning up for his first number, he said to the men simply: "I don't know what you expect to hear me play, but I do know I'm going to play Bach." He played Bach—and the G.I.'s loved it. During the next two years, in his performances for the troops in three theaters of operations (he was with the Ninth Army when it streaked towards Berlin in 1945) he always included the greatest music on his programs.

On the occasion of the thirtieth anniversary of his American début, in 1947, Heifetz announced that he would take a sabbatical from concert work. In these thirty years he had traveled more than 2,000,000 miles and had played the violin nearly 100,000 hours ("the equivalent," he has computed "of over ten years of playing twenty-four hours a day"). The time had come, he felt, to take stock of himself as an artist. "It will be like overhauling an engine," he explained, "some parts have to be changed, and some lubricated." After a year of retirement, Heifetz returned to his concert work in January 1949. Listening to him play, after the hiatus of one year, one was reminded of what Deems Taylor once said of him: "He has only one rival, one violinist whom he is trying to beat: Jascha Heifetz."

3

YEHUDI MENUHIN

◇◇

IT WAS during two years of retirement and study on a ranch in the Santa Cruz Mountains of California that Yehudi Menuhin passed through his transition from prodigy violinist to full-fledged artist. His adolescence was late. From precocity he stepped into complete maturity, and man's estate became his on the day when, in London, he married his first wife, Nola Nicholas of Australia.

The step from childhood to maturity has proved fatal for too many prodigies. It has plunged them from fame into obscurity; public adulation has become public indifference. For Yehudi, on the contrary, manhood has held no terrors. After his phenomenal début, with each year he has found himself more securely established in fame, more maturely developed as an artist. With each year, his march through the world of music has become a greater personal triumph. When, in 1937, he returned to the concert stage after an absence of two years, he illustrated once again his enormous appeal. At the box-office he established himself as one of the greatest musical attractions in the world! Artistically, he thrived equally well. The outstanding music critics, musicians, violin teachers hailed him as one of the foremost masters of his instrument.

Truth to tell, Yehudi Menuhin, the man, may no longer

be looked upon as the picturesque, chubby child prodigy whose audiences were delighted at the sight of a mere fledgling playing great music on a violin too large for him. But he has become something infinitely more important: he has become a great artist.

Today, Yehudi finds himself a world figure in music. His fame spans the globe. His career has been studded with enough triumphs to pack the normal lifetime of any other artist. On which of his many victories does this young artist today look back with the most exhilaration and nostalgia?

Was it to that all-important first appearance in New York when, as a mere child, he played the Beethoven concerto in Carnegie Hall and in Mecca Temple with the New York Symphony Society? Dressed in a white shirt with short sleeves, velvet knee-breeches, socks and pumps, he was an unforgettable sight as he gave his violin to the concertmaster for tuning. He saw ladies in the boxes sobbing softly into their handkerchiefs as, with chubby fingers, he drew exquisite sounds from his violin. He saw three thousand people rise spontaneously at the end of his performance to cheer him. He was lifted high, and kissed, by the conductor of the orchestra—Fritz Busch. . . . And the following morning, the critics joined in one chorus of praise to his genius. "When the bow touched the strings, it was evident that an exceptional musical intelligence and sensibility were behind the performance. . . . He felt, he conveyed very beautifully, the poetry of the slow movement, and his playing of the finale was of refreshing taste and simplicity," wrote Olin Downes in the *New York Times*. "From the fingers of this child of ten," wrote Samuel Chotzinoff, "the Beethoven Concerto flowed in all its nobility, its repose, its thoughtful and subjective beauty. . . ."

Is it to his unforgettable début in Berlin that Yehudi, today, most frequently turns his roving memory? Rumors of his remarkable exploits had reached Berlin, but musicians and critics were incredulous; they would have to hear for themselves. He performed at one concert three of the most difficult concertos in musical literature (those of Beethoven and Brahms and one by Bach). There were tears and cheers and rapturous enthusiasm. Some went so far as to say that they had not heard such playing since the days of Joachim. . . . But that début was especially memorable to him for quite another reason. After the concert a little man with electric eyes and bushy hair came to him backstage, lifted him high in his arms, and kissed him squarely on his hot cheek. "Today, Yehudi," the stranger said to him, "you have once again proved to me that there is a God in heaven!" The little man was Albert Einstein.

Or does Yehudi regard November 14, 1931, as the most memorable day of his life? It was then that, at the invitation of the city of Leipzig, he appeared with the Gewandhaus Orchestra on the occasion of the 150th anniversary of the great orchestra's origin. I shall let a letter from Yehudi's father, Moshe—written to a personal friend shortly after the event—describe that day of triumph.

"After Yehudi had finished performing the Mendelssohn concerto, Bruno Walter, the conductor of the orchestra, was caught speechless, holding his hand to his heart. Finally, Mr. Walter cried out aloud: 'This is a miracle! This is godlike! This is genius of the highest order!'

At the same time, the public was calling out 'Yehudi' more than twenty times, and compelled him to play an encore (the very first time in the history of symphony concerts in the Gewandhaus that an encore was given!). Yehudi played a Bach solo sonata as an encore, another thing that broke all rules. . . .

A banquet was tendered Yehudi last night, at the house of the president of the Gewandhaus, at which over one hundred of Germany's greatest leaders in art, science, music, and politics came to do him honor. The great Felix Mendelssohn's grandchildren were there to thank Yehudi for his performance of their grandfather's concerto. Dr. Bumke, vice president of the German republic and president of the Supreme Court of Germany, was there, and delivered a speech which made my spine shiver. 'Do you know, sir,' said he to me, 'that this is the very first time in my life, and I am sure in the lives of all those here present, that we have really and actually come into contact with God's greatest phenomenon of nature, the greatest genius of music that probably ever lived on earth? We are grateful to you, Yehudi's parents!' There was at this reception also Prof. Sturbe, the one who now occupies Johann Sebastian Bach's position at the Thomaskirche in Leipzig. He said simply: 'This is the greatest concert I have ever heard in my life!' "

Yehudi can look back to the time when, ill in Brussels, he was nursed by the Queen of the Belgians, the late Queen Astrid, who treated him as if he were her own child. Or to the time in Rumania when he practiced in Enesco's studio before Queen Marie, and she embraced him and autographed one of her own books for him.

Or he can reflect upon his personal contacts with the great figures of music of our day, personal contacts which soon developed into warm friendship—with Sir Edward Elgar, Bruno Walter, Hubay, Respighi, Pizzetti, Enesco.

Finally, in the fall of 1944, (after having given more than 500 concerts for the armed forces all over the world), he had the unique personal satisfaction of being the first major artist to give a concert in liberated Paris, on which occasion (appropriately enough) he played the work of a Jew, the Mendelssohn concerto. During this tour, he also

Yehudi Menuhin

gave concerts in Antwerp, only a few days after that port had been freed, and in Aachen, a stone's throw from what was then the actual front, to the accompaniment of booming artillery.

Which of these many and varied experiences has proved the most thrilling to Yehudi himself? His answer is indicative of his true personality.

"Perhaps I'm sentimental," he has said, "but the most thrilling experience I've ever had was a kiss that Maestro Toscanini gave me when he heard me play for the first time. That moment will linger in my memory longer, I think, than any of my successes in Europe and America."

Then, somewhat diffidently (he always talks about himself diffidently), Yehudi will tell you his story.

"I have worshiped Toscanini ever since the first time I heard him conduct. That's why it pained me when I learned that the Maestro consistently refused to hear me play. My former teacher, Adolph Busch—who is a very close friend of Toscanini—begged him to listen to me. But the Maestro always closed his eyes with horror, screwed his face with pain, and cried out: 'Prodigies? They all make me sick inside!' It was more than two years of persistent entreaty on the part of Adolph Busch that finally persuaded Toscanini to come to hear me. I did not know that the Maestro was in the hall. At the end of the concert, I felt myself suddenly seized and kissed. I looked up, and my heart stood still as I looked into the fiery eyes of the great conductor. He was shouting at me in Italian, at the top of his high-pitched voice: 'You are divine, Yehudi, you are divine! There is no other violinist quite like you!' And ever since that time the Maestro and I have been the very best of friends."

Certain phases of the friendship of Toscanini and Yehudi have been widely publicized, such as their trip together on the *Ile de France* some years ago when Toscanini listened to Yehudi practice for hours. "You know," Toscanini said, when the trip came to a close, "I think I've heard more good music on this trip than in all the rest of my life."

But the whole story of their friendship has, I believe, never before been told. On one occasion, Yehudi visited the Maestro several times at his home in Italy and talked music with him. One morning he asked Toscanini, "Maestro, did you ever hear the Mozart Seventh Violin Concerto?" "No, *caro* Yehudi," answered Toscanini. "You must be mistaken. Mozart composed only six violin concertos." "But, Maestro," Yehudi insisted, "Mozart composed *seven* concertos, and the seventh is probably the most mature and greatest of them all—even though the violinists ignore it." Then Yehudi took out the score, over which Maestro Toscanini pored while Yehudi played it for him. In the midst of the slow movement, the telephone rang. Impetuously, Toscanini left his seat, tore the telephone wires out of the wall, and then quietly said: "Now, *caro* Yehudi, we can make music without any disturbances!"

In New York City, for weeks at a time, Yehudi and Toscanini would discourse on music at the Hotel Astor. Frequently, Yehudi would play for Toscanini, and the Maestro would cry out in Italian that the boy played miraculously.

"But Maestro," Yehudi once complained with sincerity, "you never correct me when I play. Why don't you tell me when I play badly?"

"There's never anything wrong with your playing, Yehudi," Toscanini answered simply. "It's always perfect."

An artist's life is crowded with activity, especially if he is a box-office attraction like Menuhin. However, Yehudi

always finds several months in which he can escape far
from the madding crowd of recitals, travel, and social engagements. During these months he secludes himself, with
his family, on his large California ranch, a few miles from
his parents' home. Here diversions are few and far between. Life is well ordered and methodical. So many hours
each day are devoted to the serious study of new musical
works; so many hours belong to the reading of good books;
so many hours are occupied by rest, play, and physical
exercise—swimming in the private pool, roaming the lonely
mountain trails, horseback riding, driving or camping in
the enchanting surroundings of the Pacific Coast, or just
lounging lazily in the sun and playing with the kids.

Menuhin's parental home boasted an extraordinary combination of individuals. Besides Yehudi, the family includes two girls, both remarkably talented. Hephzibah
made her mark as a concert pianist in distinguished sonata
recitals with her brother (the most successful and the most
celebrated brother-and-sister team in music), as well as in
solo appearances, but she has sacrificed a concert career for
a happy domestic life with her husband and child in Australia. Yaltah, the youngest of the trio, has literary talent
and is a good musician, but, like her sister, prefers the retired life of wife and mother to that of a professional.

In some respects, I think, the Menuhin parents are the
most remarkable of this astonishing family. They were
both schoolteachers (neither of them, incidentally, is a
musician) with excellent cultural backgrounds. They possess intelligence, tact, and wisdom in the rearing of children, which is almost an instinct with them. Raising
children is always a precarious task. What, then, must it
be to raise a genius and two extraordinarily gifted girls?
Yet the Menuhins have performed this difficult task ad-
mirably. They balanced their children's intellectual diet

so that it might include courses other than music, and watched over their physical, as well as their mental, development. They never spoiled or pampered the children, guarding them carefully from too much praise. As a result, the three young people today glow with physical and mental health, are integrated and well-adjusted personalities.

Yehudi, as a young man, is well developed physically. He is broad-shouldered, well built, muscular and robust, alive with health and vitality. His eyes are fresh and alert; his cheeks, florid and smooth; his body, well disciplined. His mind, moreover, equals his muscles in resiliency. He speaks and writes in six languages sufficiently well, reads much in all of them. His is an unusual intellectual curiosity, a wide intellectual span. He can discuss art or politics with grace and penetration. As a matter of fact, he only rarely discusses music. I have been at the dinner table of the Menuhins when there was no discussion of music at all, politics, social questions, or literature being the principal subjects. On all such topics Yehudi and his sisters talk freely, and their ideas are often not only pertinent but also strikingly illuminating.

As a person, Yehudi impressed me most because of his quiet and dignified modesty. Although fully aware of his powers as an artist, he remains surprisingly unassuming. He almost never mentions his successes; and, if the conversation turns to them, he grows as flustered as a schoolboy listening to words of praise. When young, he never grumbled at having usually to be in bed well before midnight, nor complained because he got no greater consideration or concessions than his sisters. Today, he is still well balanced, unspoiled. I have never known him to be temperamental or hot-headed. He is as equable and completely imperturbable in everyday life as he is on the concert platform. And his complete indifference to money is as charm-

ing as it is unusual. He began signing his own checks only
after his twenty-first birthday, and only because his father
felt that the time had come to give him a sense of financial
responsibility. But his tastes are simple, and he spends his
income sparingly. I have often talked with Yehudi, but
not once have I heard him measure his success (as so many
other artists do) by the box-office yardstick.

Although he has never played ball—unless ping-pong or
badminton is considered a ball game—Yehudi is not in-
different to sports. He is enormously fond of swimming.
His bicycle was his best friend during his boyhood, and
still is. The mountain trails in California often find him
and his wife pedaling for miles. He is passionately fond
of motoring. But his greatest delight, particularly when he
was younger, was mechanics. Once he was motoring in
France when his car broke down suddenly. "Good!" he
cried out. "I hope the car's broken. Then I'll have a
chance to fix it." He lifted the hood and then, with undisguised glee, went about the task of adjusting the motor.
When he had completed the repairs, he jumped back into
the car—dirty-faced, greasy, smudged—saying wistfully,
"Too bad it wasn't a harder job!"

It should not be necessary here to describe Yehudi's life
in detail. A few of the essential facts, however, might not
be out of place. He was born in New York on April 22,
1916. A spurious article, published under his mother's
name, in a magazine of national circulation, has questioned his racial origin. Any such question is absurd. Both
Yehudi's parents are Jewish. His father, born in Russia
and raised in Palestine, was a teacher in Hebrew schools
in New York and San Francisco; his mother, though of
Tatar extraction on her father's side, has had Jewish ante-
cedents for several generations.

When Yehudi was nine months old, his parents left for

San Francisco, where the father was given a position as superintendent of the Jewish Educational Society. In San Francisco Yehudi heard his first concert. He was not a year old, and he had been taken to the concert of the San Francisco Symphony Orchestra only because his parents could not afford the cost of a nurse. To the amazement of his parents, and of those sitting near them, Yehudi was deathly still while the concert was in progress. He was taken to other concerts, and always he seemed to listen with breathless attention.

Those were the first indications of an unusual musical instinct. Another—and a much more forceful one—came when he was three years old. He was given a toy violin, and when he tried it and discovered it to be only a toy, he threw it on the floor in anger.

Soon after this incident he received a real violin, and when he had mastered the elements, he performed at a public concert conducted by the Pacific Musical Society of San Francisco. When he was four he took his first lessons from Sigmund Anker; a year and a half later, Louis Persinger—concertmaster of the San Francisco Symphony Orchestra—became his teacher. From that moment on, the playing of the violin ceased to be mere play for Yehudi and became a serious business. His application to study was extraordinary; he seemed never to grow tired of practicing. And he learned with phenomenal rapidity. When he was six, he was ready for concert appearances. He played the Mendelssohn Concerto at the Civic Auditorium in San Francisco before an audience of 9,000—and his playing was nothing short of sensational. This performance, so maturely thought out and so intelligently presented, was publicized throughout the country, and a New York engagement was immediately arranged. A few months later, the child gave his historic reading of the Beethoven concerto at Mecca Temple.

That he was not just another prodigy was evident from the very first. It was even more convincingly proved as his career began to unfold. He was a profound artist, with integrity, taste, and a high artistic standard to which he clung tenaciously. That he made his official débuts in San Francisco and New York with two great concertos instead of meretricious pieces was but the first indication that only the highest plane of art was to be his sphere. This became even more evident in later concerts—when he chose, as encores, no fussy trifles, but the solo sonatas of Bach; when (as in many of his European appearances) his program consisted entirely of three major concertos; when (as in the case of the Bach music and the Paganini concerto) he refused to follow the groove laid out by all violinists before his time—i.e. performing edited versions, but instead went to the original (*Urtext*) editions and played the music as the composers had intended it to be played; when, allowing his vein for experiment full scope, he performed great works of music rarely or never heard before— the *Adelaide Concerto* of Mozart, and the so-called "lost" concerto of Schumann; when he revealed his profound devotion to Bach by invariably including on a program either a sonata or a partita by the Leipzig master.

How to explain Yehudi's genius? He seems to have been born with music in him; his musical expression is guided by a sixth sense that has often proved infallible. His teachers confess that they have learned as much from him as he from them. Instinctively, he has always felt how a certain passage should be performed. Where the interpretation of a phrase, a nuance, the molding of a line, is concerned, there is not much that he could be taught. He seemed to be controlled by forces that none could analyze. Louis Persinger, his first important teacher, once said that at the age of eight Yehudi already had a clear and organized conception of the Beethoven concerto, and that his interpretation was in many respects as integrated as that of many a mature artist. It seems that Yehudi's interpretations spring from an inexhaustible inspiration deep within him. Once it was said to him that on two successive occasions he gave two altogether different interpretations of a Mozart sonata. "What of it?" Yehudi asked with surprise. "I felt the work differently on the second day, and so I played it differently." In words such as these you find a true artist.

Yehudi has been fortunate to have come under the influence of the great composer, violinist, conductor, and teacher, Georges Enesco. Under Enesco, Yehudi's genius ripened, and Yehudi regards him as his greatest friend— and his greatest single influence.

Today, Yehudi combines his instinct, his inspiration, his inborn taste and judgment with maturity, education, and disciplined emotions. A combination such as this is always the formula for producing a truly great musical performance. When we listen to Menuhin play a sonata of Bach or Mozart with the most exquisite sensitivity of tonal design, with an inborn feeling for musical values, and with (at certain moments) a conception that is almost other-worldly, we are tempted to say of him what one critic once said of another great artist: "He is, after all, the greatest artist on his instrument, because the way *he* plays *certain* things nobody *else* can play *anything!*"

4

NATHAN MILSTEIN

◇◇

THOUGH MILSTEIN has passed his forty-fifth birthday, he retains his youthful appearance almost magically. In the twenty years he has been concertizing in this country, he has not changed very markedly. Now, as then, his hair is dark, his eyes have an intriguing sparkle, the lines of his face are soft, and over it hovers an expression of freshness.

He has about him, too, an engaging quality of boyishness. What he does, he does with gusto, whether it is eating Viennese pastry, buying a new set of brilliantly colored silk pajamas, indulging in games of bridge, gin rummy, or ping-pong (in all three of which he is adept). His favorite hobby, painting watercolors, is undertaken with zest. ("On days of concerts," he explains, "I do more painting than practicing the violin.") So are the innumerable chores demanding his attention on his 150-year old Colonial farm in Vermont.

Boyish, too, is the way in which he remains a victim of a long catalogue of superstitions: He always carries with him, as a good-luck charm, a watch that was presented to him as a concert fee in revolution-torn Russia; he always goes around a lamppost on the right side, and in crossing a

street he will detour around a parked car rather than pass
it on the left.

This seemingly inexhaustible youthfulness—which is
not to be interpreted as immaturity—is to be found in his
music, too. There is freshness, zest, enthusiasm in his playing. It is the playing of a man in love with what he is doing.
It is these qualities that have endeared him to his large
public: Milstein is not for the small, esoteric circle of
connoisseurs.

Born in Odessa on December 31, 1904, the son of a
wealthy wool importer, Milstein studied the violin first
with Stoliarsky, then with such masters as Eugène Ysaÿe
and Leopold Auer. During the first turbulent years of
revolution, he concertized extensively through Russia. At
the same time he used to join in performances of chamber
music with two other young musicians then still unknown
but later to become world famous—the pianist Vladimir
Horowitz and the 'cellist Gregor Piatigorsky; the three
have remained bosom friends ever since.

In 1925, Milstein was compelled to leave Russia. He
went to Paris, arriving there without friends, money, influence, or even a violin. It was not long before generous
patrons were attracted to his talent and stood ready to help
him. One of them financed his Paris début; another provided a Stradivarius. That concert was sensational, and
engagements were thenceforth not difficult to get, not only
in France, but in the rest of Europe as well. Within three
years, Milstein had established himself in Europe as one
of the favorite concert artists of the day.

In the fall of 1928, he came to the United States, making his American début as soloist with the Philadelphia
Orchestra conducted by Stokowski. His extraordinary technical powers excited American audiences, just as his

warmth and intensity thrilled them. It was not long before he was filling a hundred engagements a season in this country, and before crowded auditoriums.

What was most impressive about Milstein, when he first came here, was his technical equipment, his sensuous tone, and the romantic glow of his interpretations. What he lacked was discipline, restraint, scholarship. Since 1928, however, he has grown formidably—his musical perception keener, his artistic sensibilities more refined, his insight more profound, his conceptions more mature. If today his Tchaikovsky concerto is still as passionate a reading of this masterpiece as is known, his interpretation of a Bach solo sonata on the other hand has stateliness, majesty, and quiet introspection. Milstein has learned to keep his youthful passions curbed by a trenchant intellect, and, in learning this, he has joined the ranks of our greatest violinists. The critic of the New York *Times* emphasized this not long ago in pointing out that "now there is plainly at work a new and deeper impulse, a probing for something far beyond the mere attractiveness of sprightly tempi, vigorous accents, and bright technique."

5

JOSEPH SZIGETI

◇◇◇

J OSEPH SZIGETI represents the opposite pole in the art of violin-playing to Nathan Milstein. Szigeti is primarily cerebral; Milstein is emotional. Each is in his own right a consummate artist whose playing affords immeasurable delight; but each is king in his own realm. If we would prefer Szigeti in a performance of Mozart or Brahms, we would just as readily concede that in Tchaikovsky it is Milstein who is incomparable.

The art of Joseph Joachim, fabulous violinist of another age, is today most closely approximated in the playing of Szigeti. Curiously enough, Szigeti—like his distinguished predecessor—is Hungarian by nationality and Jewish by religion; and, paradoxically, both are characteristically un-Hungarian and un-Jewish in their art. With the Hungarian, we associate the hot blood of the *csardas;* with the Jew, indulgence in emotion and sentiment. Yet Szigeti—like Joachim before him—is most strongly guided, not by emotional impulses, but by his keen and trenchant intellect. His performance is always a studied art, as carefully and fastidiously conceived in every detail as a symphony in the hands of a great conductor.

While there is no question that a great deal of trenchant analysis goes into all the performances of Milstein also, it

is the emotional impulse of his playing that moves us most
profoundly. A Milstein concert has the warm blood of
youth. It is passionate, intense, ardent.

It may be recalled that when Joachim visited Russia at
the prime of his career, he was greeted with reserve that
approached apathy. To Russian music lovers, accustomed
to the heady wine of Wieniawski, Joachim's playing was
as frigid, as coldly calculated, as the solo sonatas of Bach
which he had resurrected and which, to the Russians at
the time, seemed downright boring. It may be recalled
that, similarly, when Szigeti gave his first concerts in
America he was often greeted coldly. His tone, some said,
lacked the human quality of tenderness; his style was too
restrained and reserved; he held his emotions too much in
check; he was—in short—too much the mind, too little the
heart.

To some of us who consider Szigeti an artist of the first
importance, one of whom we are proudest, such accusa-
tions are as unjustified as those leveled at Joachim in
Russia. We consider Szigeti in a class by himself. An art
such as his—so penetratingly analytical, so beautifully
sculptured in every line and curve—can never have a mass
appeal. Essentially, Szigeti's art is for the discriminating.
He is—so they will tell you—a violinist's violinist.

If, when he plays at Carnegie Hall, he does not pack the
hall to the doors as one or two other violinists do, he can
at least boast of having a most fastidious audience before
him. Concert violinists are there in droves, to study his
style in all its varied subtleties, to derive, through his insight, a new conception of great violin music.

They know that at Szigeti's concerts they will hear programs that are musically significant throughout, programs
that never cater to popular taste, that are intelligently balanced, including the dessert of novelty with the roast beef

of classical music. For Szigeti, more than any other violinist since Joachim, has made an art of program-building;
few concert violinists will deny that he has profoundly
influenced that art.

A Szigeti program is always an adventure for the music
lover. At one time, in New York, he gave a series of concerts that spanned the history of violin music; avenues in
violin music, long closed, were then opened. Such rarities
as a *Divertimento* by Mozart (who had ever heard of a
violinist featuring an orchestral *Divertimento* on a recital
program?), and a hitherto unknown concerto by Tartini
were introduced at another of his recitals, with the assistance of a chamber orchestra. At still another concert he
invited Benny Goodman to appear with him for the world
première of Béla Bartók's *Rhapsody* for clarinet, violin
and piano. These are only a few indications that a Szigeti
program is always alive, novel, and ingeniously contrived.

Concert violinists who come to Szigeti's concerts understand that if, as in the Brahms concerto, Szigeti adopts a
style that is acrid and harsh, it is only because he has
found in the work a strength and toughness of fiber; and
also that he can play Schubert with sensuous and soaring
lyricism. In certain modern works, Szigeti's playing actually approaches the ugly, in the stridency of tones he pro-
duces on the violin—as, for example, in the first Prokofiev
violin concerto, which he introduced to the world, and of
which he is (as Prokofiev himself has said) the greatest
interpreter. But in the classical sonata he is a purist, ad-
hering strictly to the classical line. And in the classical
sonata, Szigeti adopts a chamber-music style in which the
virtuoso is forgotten in the mutual adjustment of the two
instruments.

In short, concert violinists understand that Szigeti's
style changes miraculously almost with every composition.

For technique, to him, does not consist merely in the ability to produce a full rich tone, or to play a complicated passage with neatness of execution. It is much more than that: it is the ability to adapt his equipment to the different styles of different composers.

The type of audience that comes to hear Szigeti play is a tribute to his art. An equally eloquent tribute is the eagerness with which modern composers prepare works especially for him. Hamilton Harty and Alfredo Casella have dedicated their violin concertos to him; Busoni's is permanently associated with his name. Dedications to him likewise appear on Eugène Ysaÿe's violin sonata, Bloch's *Nuit exotique,* Templeton Strong's *Poem,* Saminsky's *Hamavdil,* Béla Bartók's *Rhapsody* for violin and orchestra and his *Rhapsody* for clarinet, violin, and piano (the last-named, jointly, to him and Benny Goodman), Joseph Achron's *Stempenyu Suite,* Alexander Tansman's *Suite,* and Prokofiev's *Chant sans paroles.* Ernest Bloch waited more than a year for the world première of his violin concerto so that Szigeti might give it its first performance.

For the great modern composers realize that when Szigeti plays their music, their inmost fancy, their slightest intentions, become fully realized; that their music is not exploited for the glorification of the artist and his technique, but that artist and technique become the humble servants of the music.

Look at the man; notice his fine and sensitive face, the high, majestic forehead whose height is accentuated by the sparse growth of hair, the far-seeing eyes, the soft slopes of the cheek. Talk to him, listen to him discourse on aesthetics, science, or literature . . . and you will gain an insight into the aristocratic personality which is the source of his profound and moving art.

His height gives him a suggestion of awkwardness, even

when he is on the platform. But, as you watch him more closely, you notice that his body is lithe and supple, and his gestures (particularly those of his hands) are graceful. As he talks to you, he speaks in a soft, well-modulated voice, which he never raises even when excited. He likes to talk, and—at the slightest provocation—will grow expansive over some beautiful painting he has seen, a great book he has read, his most recent travels, or the aviary of exotic birds he keeps at his beautiful home in Palos Verdes, California.

Szigeti knew two great musical influences early in his career, and to these he freely expresses his indebtedness. One was the violinist Joseph Joachim, whom he heard play when he was very young; this was an experience that Szigeti never forgot. The other was the great pianist, composer, and conductor, Ferruccio Busoni, at one time a personal friend of Szigeti. These two great artists—their integrity, their idealism, their intellectual approach to their art—directed Szigeti's artistic course.

Szigeti has also acknowledged indebtedness to Béla Bartók. The folk elements in Bartók's compositions have exerted a strong influence on Szigeti, who has transcribed some of Bartók's Hungarian folk-tunes for the violin. Szigeti has frequently appeared in joint recitals with Bartók, both in Europe and in America, in programs featuring the composer's music.

Joseph Szigeti was born in Budapest on September 5, 1892. Showing an early aptitude for the violin, he was given instruction first by his father and then by his uncle. He outgrew these preliminary studies quickly, and was placed under the expert guidance of the great Hungarian violinist and teacher, Jenö Hubay.

When Szigeti was twelve years old, his teacher brought

Nathan Milstein

him to the great Joachim, who accompanied the boy at the piano as he played the Beethoven violin concerto. The performance was sufficiently distinguished for Joachim to encourage him in an artistic career. One year later, Szigeti made his début at the Royal Academy of Budapest. And two years after that, at the age of fifteen, he played in Berlin and Dresden, and finally came to England.

Here Szigeti remained for six years, concertizing extensively in London and the provinces, sometimes in joint recitals with the singer Melba, the pianist Bachaus, and the great composer Busoni. Szigeti's playing received praise throughout England. "He has the *diablerie* which must have been Paganini's secret," the London *Times* wrote. Another critic compared his interpretations to a Benvenuto Cellini masterpiece, in its perfect balance and beauty.

In 1912, Szigeti's concert tour brought him out of England to Berlin and Paris, where he successfully featured the Busoni violin concerto, dedicated to him by the composer. In Paris his concert was organized by the foremost intellectual figures then in the city, including Gabriele d'Annunzio, Isidor Philipp, Moritz Moszkowski, Charles Widor, and Rainer Maria Rilke. After the concert (at which the chief work was once again the Busoni concerto), a banquet took place at the old café-restaurant Henri. A piano was brought to the first floor, and there—when the dinner was over—Busoni played his formidable piano work, the *Fantasia Contrappuntistica,* to his many disciples.

Szigeti's concert tour continued. His reputation grew, not by sudden inflation, but slowly and steadily. His beautiful conceptions were talked of, and his exquisite etchings of the great musical works.

In 1917, Szigeti succeeded the celebrated Henri Marteau

as professor of the course in violin virtuosity at the Geneva Conservatory. He held his position with distinction until 1924.

Leopold Stokowski, then conductor of the Philadelphia Orchestra, heard him play in Europe and invited him to America. In the autumn of 1925, Szigeti made his début as soloist with that orchestra in Philadelphia, playing the concerto of Beethoven. A week later, he repeated this performance in New York.

Some of the critics were cool because his tone lacked the fullness and wealth of Heifetz's, and his interpretation lacked the charm of Kreisler's. But a few recognized that he was an individualist who must not be measured by the yardstick of existing standards, that his style was uniquely his own. They realized that, with Szigeti, the design of the music, the musical content of a composition, were of first importance—not the minute elements of violin-playing. Olin Downes compared Szigeti to Eugène Ysaÿe because of his "breadth and generosity of style." Another critic proclaimed him "an individuality—a violinist whose art is more than an episode of a season."

But it would be wrong to call Szigeti's début in America sensational. He was not immediately numbered among the elect of contemporary violinists—except by a limited handful of discerning music lovers. Passing seasons, however, brought renewed contact with Szigeti's art, and renewed contact disclosed the infinite variety of his playing and the true nobility of his interpretations. He was, it was soon learned, the consummate artist who, as Paul Stefan pointed out, "represents with equal completeness the classic greatness and the modern spirit of violin-playing."

Szigeti has his devoted followers throughout the world. His audience exists wherever music is played. His concert tours are extensive: from May 1931 to May 1933, for example, he circled the globe twice, giving more than two hundred performances. In Tokio, he played five consecutive nights; and seven consecutive nights in Buenos Aires. He was invited twelve times to the Soviet Union, where he has been accorded one of the greatest receptions. In 1938, he was so triumphantly received in South Africa that a schedule of twelve concerts was expanded to nineteen.

The foremost honors have fallen to him. In France, he was awarded the Legion of Honor. In Belgium, he was made Commander of the Order of Leopold. He has received the Officer's Cross of the Hungarian *Ordre pour le mérite*. In Japan—before Pearl Harbor, of course—he was the recipient of the Jiji Shimpo Gold Medal.

But perhaps the greatest honor that is his is the devoted enthusiasm of his followers, musicians who remain stanchly faithful to him, who hear him whenever he chooses to play, and who derive from his playing an aesthetic pleasure, such as they get only from a handful of living artists.

IV

'CELLISTS

1. *Pablo Casals*
2. *Gregor Piatigorsky*

1

PABLO CASALS

◇◇

W<small>HEN</small>, in the summer of 1936, Civil War broke out in Spain, friends of Pablo Casals urged him to leave Barcelona and carry on his art in quieter and more grateful surroundings. To such entreaties, Casals made an answer characteristic of him. In these difficult hours, he said, the Spanish people needed music more than ever before. It was unthinkable for him to desert his people now that they could turn to art to succor them and give them spiritual strength.

If he were to leave for other European capitals, it would be for one reason alone: he would concertize in order to raise money for Spain, to help his country materially, as well as spiritually, in its war against Fascist invasion.

And so, with his native Spain torn and bleeding, Casals summoned his art to help his people. He played extensively in France and England so that the money he earned might be translated into sadly needed food, clothing, and supplies. Between tours he returned to Barcelona to continue conducting his famous concerts of symphonic music, and playing his violoncello. The city might be paralyzed by war. Bombs from Italian planes might drop perilously near the concert hall. Scarcity of food might raise the gruesome specter of starvation. The hospitals might be filled with the crippled and the dying, many of them non-combatants, innocent victims of foreign air attacks. But music in Spain went on to capacity audiences, because their director felt that Spain needed a spiritual haven from madness.

Casals' career as an artist has been marked by other similar gestures of self-denial and nobility. His greatness as a human being is comparable only to his stature as an artist. Those who know him well—and I have talked with some of his intimate friends—speak of his ascetic simplicity, his directness, his scrupulous honesty, and, above all else, the rich vein of nobility in him.

Long before 1936—in happier days for Spain—he showed his allegiance to his country and his devotion to his people. The foundation of his world-famous Orquesta Pau Casals is a significant example.

Barcelona had had symphony orchestras before, but always their life span was brief. It was said that Catalonians were too poor to support a permanent symphony orchestra. More important still, it was said that they were too unmusical to appreciate one.

Casals lamented Barcelona's lack of so important a cultural influence as a permanent orchestra. He made contact with important musicians, patrons, and government officials, and urged the formation of a good symphonic organization on a permanent basis. But wherever he went he met with pessimism. It was a hopeless dream, he was told. Catalonians simply were not interested in great music. For their tastes, café-house orchestras were ample.

But Casals did not admit defeat. He had money, and his violoncello brought him a substantial income. He had important artistic connections. He decided that, on his own responsibility, he would organize a permanent symphony orchestra in Barcelona. He combed the city for the best musicians available, guaranteed them their salaries from his own pocketbook, and set to work.

The difficulties which then faced Casals were heart-breaking, and would have destroyed a spirit less defiant than his. Political differences among the musicians almost disrupted the newborn organization; only the infinite tact of the conductor smoothed over differences of opinion. Musical problems were even more formidable. Some of the musicians had never played in an orchestra. To co-ordinate their work, to organize them into a unified body —in some cases even to teach them the essential technique —required Herculean work on the part of Casals, particu-larly since, from the very first, he insisted on addressing himself only to the greatest music. He worked so slavishly and with such undivided concentration that, at one time, he broke down physically and was forced to rest for a while.

Finally, the first concert took place, on October 13, 1920, at the Music Auditorium of the Catalan Palace. The re-sponse to the new orchestra was at first cool. But Casals had faith in his cause. He continued defraying all the expenses. He continued his fastidious preparation for each concert. Then, slowly, subscriptions began to increase; the hall grew more and more crowded. At last, there were capacity audiences—Casals' orchestra had achieved perma-nency.

Having achieved what so many had said was impossible— the establishment of a great orchestra in Barcelona—Casals was not satisfied. He was soon fired with another and still greater ambition. He wanted great music to reach not only the persons who could pay the price, but also the lowest-paid workmen of Barcelona, to whom the price of admis-sion to concerts was prohibitive. Early in his life, Casals had read Karl Marx passionately; and from then on, his humanitarian interest in the underdog of society never deserted him. Now he wished to translate theory into practice—to do something tangible and important for the workers: bring them great music, the greatest music, at prices they could afford.

Once again, Casals was faced with staggering difficulties (not the least of which was the skepticism of the workers themselves, who suspected anyone who brought them something for nothing). Once again he encountered argument and discouragement which would have disheartened many another. But once again he triumphed over difficulties through the sheer force of his will. He evolved a musical organization for workers which, for a few cents, entitled them to participation in a variety of musical activities, including attendance at six Sunday morning concerts of Casals' orchestra. For these concerts, Casals maintained a rigorously high artistic standard, and was often inspired by the magnificent reception his music received from the workers.

About Casals' conducting, Mr. Fox-Strangways, distinguished critic of the London *Observer*, wrote:

"He plays as if he held a responsible trust, determined that at all costs the purity of the faith shall not suffer at his hands. He refrains from anything histrionic or ephemeral; he wants the truth of it. So the tempi of Beethoven's Seventh Symphony were what excitable people call 'dry.' They do not realize how much they have destroyed Beethoven and Brahms for us by their fussy sentimentality, and that the only way to get these back is to mean every word of them, as he does. . . . In whatever he does, he seems to aim at some invisible and unattainable ideal, and if some part of that is reached immediately to set the standard higher."

However, it is as a violoncellist rather than as a conductor that Pablo Casals is, for many of us, one of the supreme artists of our time. His conducting (if I may judge him by phonograph records, since I have heard Casals conduct in public only once, and the memory of that performance is not very vivid in my mind) has the stamp of profound musicianship, integrity, taste, discipline. But it is as violoncellist that he raises the music he performs beyond sheer competence and musical authenticity, to Alpine peaks of greatness.

To many of us the memory of Casals playing the concertos of Haydn and Dvořák, or combining with Harold Bauer in a concert of Beethoven sonatas at Town Hall, or reading the Bach solo sonatas and suites in his own recitals, is a memory of experiences never to be forgotten. His technique! It is as much a part of him as breathing, and comes from him as naturally. He has evolved his own system of fingering and bowing, which makes everything he plays seem simplified. His tone! It pours from his instrument opulent but never sugary. The style! It is that of a profound scholar and an aristocrat—every effect, every shade so subtly realized that one forgets the interpreter in the contemplation of a profound artistic expression. His feeling for architectonic construction! "This magician," wrote Diran Alexanian, famous French teacher and violoncellist, "makes you anticipate what is coming in the same way that he makes you remember what is past. In his playing, every note that is not a forecast is a memory. . . . Each detail has had attention, but the details are graded according to their importance."

He is the poet of his instrument; of few artists can this be said with equal justification. One recalls, for example, his performance of the *Adagio* movement of the Haydn concerto, or of the *Adagio affettuoso* movement of the Brahms F-major sonata. Other 'cellists bring to this music a wealth of tone and feeling; but only a supreme artist like

Casals can, with the utmost reserve, without torturing a figure or retarding a phrase, convert such "poems" into piercing, tragic utterances, ennobled by simplicity of expression.

Casals has the independence and courage and integrity of the supreme artist. France was not sympathetic to the sonatas of Brahms. Nevertheless, Casals played them (the box-office notwithstanding!), and played them so frequently that France, too, learned to appreciate the beauty of the music. If a famous orchestra leader slighted his beloved Dvořák concerto and asked him to substitute something else, he preferred not appearing at all to changing the music.

Most important, however, have been Casals' efforts in bringing recognition to the great solo sonatas and suites of Johann Sebastian Bach.

While he was still in his adolescence, Casals—rummaging through some music in a second-hand shop in Barcelona—came across some copies of Bach's solo suites for violoncello. These works had almost never been performed by 'cellists, who regarded them (if they regarded them at all) as only good exercise material. To Casals, the Bach music opened a new world. From that day, Bach's music for the violoncello became his religion. He devoted his magnificent zeal and effort to studying these works, analyzing phrase by phrase, bar by bar, until he felt that he could give them the performance they required. Then, on his concert tours, he set out to spread the knowledge of this music, playing it frequently in the face of criticism, boredom, and the despair of his concert managers. He played it until, at last, the world saw through his eyes the majesty of Bach's music.

If Mendelssohn rediscovered for the world the *St. Matthew Passion* and Joseph Joachim the violin sonatas and suites, so Pablo Casals can be said to have restored to the music world the Bach solo sonatas and suites for violoncello.

The Casals family was one of the social pillars of the small Catalonian town of Vendrell, Tarragona, respected by all the townspeople. The father, Carles Casals, was a church organist, a teacher of singing and piano, and a respectable composer. He stemmed from proud Catalonian stock; the mother was also partly Catalonian.

On December 29, 1876, a second child was born to the family. He was christened Pablo. He was a musical child. From his father he received instruction in singing and composition almost in his crib, and in his fourth year he already sang in the parish church. The Gregorian chants which he heard and sang in church constituted his first strong musical impressions. At six, he supplemented his study of the piano with that of the organ and began to write music. At seven, he began the study of the violin. Playfully, Carles Casals used to tell his wife that they had been blessed with another Mozart!

This preoccupation with music did not bar Pablo from the more normal life of a child. He was small and slight, but healthy. He made friendships easily and was well liked by the children of his own age. He loved the outdoors; no less enthusiastically than his companions did he indulge in athletics—indeed, he was an excellent runner and high-jumper.

But music was a world of endless wonder to him. The farther he traveled, the more he yearned to explore.

When he was ten, there took place in his town a Christmas performance of a pastoral play. The music for this spectacle was found unsatisfactory, and Father Casals was asked to prepare a new score. For this assignment he en-

listed the collaboration of his talented young son. Together, they wrote more than a dozen musical numbers,
which became so popular that—as we are informed by
Casals' biographer, Lillian Littlehales *—some of the pieces
are still sung by the townspeople.

Shortly after this, Pablo Casals heard a violoncello for
the first time. The Catholic Center of Vendrell arranged a
concert by instrumentalists, one of whom was José Garcia,
a well-known violoncellist from Barcelona. Hardly had the
concert begun when Pablo pointed a finger at the 'cello
and urged his father to give him lessons on that instrument. Thus Pablo received his first 'cello instruction from
his father. But his progress was so swift that other instruction was necessary, and eventually it was decided to send
him to Barcelona and have him enroll at the Municipal
School where he could study not only harmony and counterpoint but also the 'cello under José Garcia himself.
Pablo was eleven years old when he entered the school.
For three years he worked hard at his studies and won
several prizes in theory and composition.

To support himself during his three years of study,
Casals joined a trio that played every evening in a café-
house outside of Barcelona—and played the usual café-
house repertoire of light music. But Pablo was even then
too fine a musician to conform rigidly to a stereotyped
repertoire. Before long he introduced in his programs
selections from the great classics. Then he prevailed upon
the manager of the café to grant him one evening a week
on which to play only the best music. That evening soon
became famous throughout Barcelona. The city's *intelli-
genzia*—musicians, writers, painters, actors—made the café-
house their weekly rendezvous on the evening when
Casals featured musical masterpieces. One of these visitors

* *Pablo Casals,* by Lillian Littlehales. New York, 1929.

was the famous Spanish composer, Isaac Albéniz, who immediately interested himself in the young musician and, from that time on, became his devoted friend.

It was at this time that Pablo Casals made his Bach discovery. At a Barcelona music shop, he was rummaging through a pile of second-hand music in his search for some good music to include on his programs, when—as he himself has written—

"my attention was suddenly arrested by some unaccompanied suites of Bach for 'cello. I forgot entirely the reason of my visit to the shop and could only stare at this music which nobody had told me about. Sometimes even now, when I look at the covers of that old music, I see again the interior of that old and musty shop with its faint smell of the sea. I took the suites home and read and reread them. For twelve years after that, I studied and worked every day at them. I was nearly twenty-five before I had the courage to play one of them in public."

Isaac Albéniz soon advised him to abandon Barcelona and go to Madrid, where there were greater opportunities for a young musician. In 1894, therefore, equipped with glowing letters of introduction from Isaac Albéniz and Fernandez Arbós, Casals left for Madrid. Here, he performed successfully at the royal palace and soon found a generous and interested patron in Count Morphy. Here, also, he studied with greater assiduity than ever before—composition under Tomás Bretón, and 'cello under Jesús de Monasterio. It was the latter who, Casals has frequently confessed, exerted the most powerful influence over his artistic growth.

Through Count Morphy, Casals received a pension from the Queen enabling him to study at Brussels under the celebrated theorist, Gevaert. Gevaert was too old to accept private pupils, and he advised Casals to proceed to

Paris. But he urged him first to visit the 'cello class at the Brussels Conservatory and play for its professor. "What can you play, my young Spaniard?" the professor asked him. "Anything," answered the young musician with cool self-assurance. The professor snickered; so did the class. "*Anything?*" The professor enumerated a few of the representative concertos for the 'cello, then some of the less famous ones. Casals said he could play them all. "Very well," said the professor acidly; "play anything you wish and show us if you are really as remarkable as you say."

Casals, in recalling this incident, remarked that the stinging tongue of the professor, coupled with the snickering and the laughter of the class, determined him to give an exceptional performance. He played as he had probably never played before. When he finished, the professor took him aside and said: "You are truly remarkable. You must study under me." To which Casals coolly answered: "I don't like you or your attitude. You have treated me so badly that I will not stay with you another minute." And without another word, he left the classroom.

He stayed two days in Brussels, and then left for Paris. If Brussels had been discouraging, what then can be said of Paris, where Casals met hardship, starvation, and apathy? For Count Morphy was displeased by the move and withdrew the pension. Through the influence of a friend, Casals secured some work in a vaudeville house, the salary from which—meager though it was—kept him from starvation. The work was taxing and undermined his strength. "Every day I had to walk miles to and from this work with my violoncello under my arm. My mother eked out with sewing a few francs. There were not only the two of us to keep but a little baby boy, too young for my mother to have left in Spain. After a few weeks, I became ill with

Gregor Piatigorsky

the strain, and there was nothing left but to return to Spain."

Back in Barcelona, Casals confronted good fortune for the first time in his life. His former teacher, José Garcia, had resigned from the Municipal School and had left for Buenos Aires. His post was now offered to Casals.

He plunged into a delirium of musical activity. He taught at the Municipal School, played the violoncello in churches, and became the first 'cellist of the Opera Orchestra in Barcelona. He formed his own string quartet, which gave successful public performances. During the summer—when musical activity relaxed in Barcelona—he played in the fashionable casino of a small Portuguese town.

At the end of one summer, on his way back from Portugal to Barcelona, Casals stopped off at Madrid where, for the first time in his career, he gave a public performance with a symphony orchestra. He performed the Lalo Concerto in D minor with Tomás Bretón conducting the orchestra. His performance was so successful that the Queen bestowed upon him the Order of Carlos III.

For two years, Casals worked hard in Barcelona, saved money, and practiced industriously on his 'cello. He was developing and growing as an artist. Then, having accumulated a comfortable bank account, he decided to abandon his work in Barcelona and to visit Paris a second time —perhaps now to enter a career as concert artist officially.

He arrived in Paris in the autumn of 1899 with a letter of introduction from Count Morphy to Charles Lamoureux, conductor of the famous orchestra bearing his name, and one of the most influential musicians in France. At the time, Lamoureux was absorbed in the work of preparing *Tristan und Isolde* for performance in Paris. When Casals arrived at Lamoureux's home, the conductor was busy working at the piano. Lamoureux interrupted his work long enough to give his visitor a casual greeting. "Come tomorrow," he said brusquely. "And bring your 'cello." The next day Casals returned and played. Lamoureux—who had not interrupted his work even while Casals was playing—suddenly raised his head from his papers. Motionless, he listened, his face beaming. At the end of Casals' performance he embraced him and exclaimed: "But you are extraordinary! You must play at my very next concert."

In October of 1899, Casals made his début in Paris with the Lamoureux Orchestra and was a sensation. Overnight, he became famous. Engagements from all parts of Europe and America poured in upon him.

A few months after this début, the man who had discovered him and first revealed him to the world, Charles Lamoureux, died. "With his death passed my days of poverty and struggle."

Thereafter, Casals' career was one of uninterrupted triumph. He concertized throughout the world—visiting America first in 1901, and then again in 1904—and saw his reputation swell prodigiously. The world soon recognized him as one of its most precious artists, and has honored him lavishly. His own government has bestowed upon him innumerable decorations and awards. From Germany he received the degree of Science and Arts; from Austria-Hungary, the Cross of the Commander of Francis Joseph; from France, the Legion of Honor, the Palme Académique, and the Cross of L'Instruction Publique; from Italy, membership in the Royal Academy of St. Cecilia of Rome; from Portugal, the order of Santiago da Espada; from Rumania, the Commandership of the Crown; and from London the Beethoven gold medal previously bestowed upon Brahms, Rubinstein, Joachim, and Liszt.

For many years, Casals divided his residence, and also the major part of his music-making, between Paris and Barcelona. In Paris, he not only gave his solo performances and sonata recitals, but also combined with Jacques Thibaud and Alfred Cortot in trio performances which were often the high points of the concert season. In Barcelona, he founded his orchestra, and shared his efforts between the 'cello and the baton.

At one time, Casals seriously thought of abandoning the 'cello. He had married the American singer, Susan Metcalfe, in 1914. For several seasons, he appeared as an accompanist to his wife in Lieder recitals. For a long time he contemplated giving up his own career to further that of his wife. But, fortunately, he never made the fatal decision.

The truth is that Casals does not like playing the 'cello, detests extensive concertizing, and would prefer to devote all his time and zeal to conducting. An interesting anecdote illustrates this. Once, climbing Mt. Tamalpais, he saw a huge rock descending upon him. He made an impetuous move to avoid the descending rock, but in doing so caught a finger of his left hand and crushed it. The first thought that came to his mind was, "Thank God, I won't have to play the 'cello again!"

Fortunately for the world of music, this accident did not end Casals' career as a 'cellist. But he has always relieved the tension and strain of concert work as a virtuoso with guest performances as a conductor. He has directed the major orchestras in Vienna, Paris, London, Rome, Berlin, Prague, Zurich, and Buenos Aires. In 1922, he conducted the New York Symphony Society at Carnegie Hall for one performance.

Conducting is no less arduous a task for Casals than

playing the 'cello; it is, as a matter of fact, an occupation that exhausts him physically and mentally. But musicianship as profound as that of Casals refuses to be hemmed in by the limited boundaries of virtuoso performances. Conducting offers Casals an inexhaustibly rich medium of self-expression, such as he cannot find in his 'cello. His ambition, therefore, is some day to make the transition from 'cello to baton complete and irrevocable.

Before that day comes, it is to be hoped that Pablo Casals returns to America to refresh our memory of his incomparable playing. It has been almost two decades since he last concertized in this country. In the intervening period, a civil war has been fought in his country—a bloody war whose Catalan victims included Pablo Casals. For a long time his friends in this country and elsewhere knew little or nothing of his fate. Then—towards the end of 1944—heartening news of him came from his eminent colleague, the violinist Jacques Thibaud. Casals had been living in seclusion in the South of France (though not—as was rumored—in a Franco concentration camp), and was in good condition. "I heard Pablo play excerpts from the Bach suites," reported Thibaud, "and he is greater than ever before." During his absence, we have heard here many admirable, even extraordinary, 'cellists. But there are no substitutes for Casals. The gap he has left in our concert life cannot be adequately filled in our time, unless he himself returns to fill it.

2

GREGOR PIATIGORSKY

◇◇

THE CRITICS have often referred to Gregor
Piatigorsky as "the Russian Casals." On the American
concert stage, no other 'cellist today has his artistic stature—certainly no one since the untimely death of Eman-
uel Feuermann. Like Casals, though to a lesser degree,
Piatigorsky is that unique blend of intellect and heart, of
scholarship and human emotion, which, together with a
consummate mastery of his instrument, bring new shadows
and perspectives to the 'cello literature. He is the virtuoso
answer to the modern composer's prayer; some of the most
important composers of our time have dedicated concertos
to him, including Hindemith, Prokofiev and Castelnuovo-
Tedesco.

In a discerning analysis of his art, Olin Downes described Piatigorsky's tone as possessing "every sonority and
shading—an organ fullness and virility; lyrical beauty and
intensity in passages of sustained song; or fine-spun as silk
in pianissimo measures or passages of rapid ornamentation.
There seems no limit to the security and agility of the
left hand or the power and variety of result with which the
bow was wielded. . . . The sentiment is noble, the line
classic, the sense of form always present. In a word, a great
virtuoso, and a greater artist. . . ."

He was born in Dnepropetrovsk, a small town in the Ukraine, on April 17, 1903. As a child, he was taught to play the 'cello by his father, a violinist. Financial disaster struck his family when the boy was only six. Obliged to help support them, the boy found a job as 'cellist in a local movie house; though his musical and academic studies were not neglected. When he was fifteen he went to Moscow, finding there a post in the orchestra of the Imperial Opera. At the same time, he continued his 'cello studies with Alfred von Glehn.

Success did not come to him so easily as to other famous virtuosos. For long there were hardships, and uncounted personal deprivations. The Revolution in Russia brought suffering, and Gregor struggled with both intense cold and hunger; we have stories of his playing in icy auditoriums while wearing his heavy fur coat, utilizing each pause in the music to warm his stiff fingers with his breath. Though he naturally thought of escaping to happier lands, he was denied a passport. In 1921, he put himself into the hands of a band of smugglers, who, for a price, promised to get him across the Polish border. They kept their promise, but not before robbing him of every possession, and Piatigorsky arrived in Warsaw, penniless and friendless. For several months his appalling poverty almost shattered his spirit. Then, suddenly, good fortune struck: substituting for a sick 'cellist at the Warsaw Opera, he was given a permanent job.

In 1923, he went to Berlin for more study. There Julius Klengel, one of the most celebrated 'cello teachers in Germany, frankly told him that he was already a master of his instrument and that there was little more he could learn. But no worthwhile opening appeared, and he played in cafés and movie houses, for wages so meager as to be hardly enough for his everyday subsistence.

Then, one day, Artur Schnabel heard him play and invited him to participate in a chamber-music performance. One of the musicians on that occasion—a flutist of the Berlin Philharmonic—was so impressed by Piatigorsky's playing that he proceeded to plead the young musician's cause with Wilhelm Furtwängler, conductor of the Philharmonic. Furtwängler advised Piatigorsky to enter a competition then being held for the post of first 'cellist in the orchestra. Piatigorsky won the competition easily; and, from that moment on, his career moved with giant strides.

Besides playing in the orchestra, he appeared as soloist, then in his own recitals. Before long, musical Berlin began to call him "the wonder 'cellist," and his popularity so increased that five wealthy Berlin music-lovers joined to buy an Amati 'cello for him—the first time that Piatigorsky had ever owned a really fine instrument. Other concerts in Europe spread his fame. In 1929, he launched his first tour of America, first at Oberlin, Ohio, on November 5, then the following month as soloist with the Philadelphia Orchestra under Stokowski and the New York Philharmonic-Symphony under Mengelberg in the Dvořák Concerto. He has since then—and practically from his first appearances—become one of the most famous 'cellists in America. He has helped, at least partially, to fill the gap left by Casals' prolonged absence. During twenty years of concert tours in this country he has given close to 1,000 recitals and has made almost 250 appearances with orchestras.

Though he is six foot three inches tall, Piatigorsky gives no impression of ungainliness either on or off the stage. A lifetime of devotion to sports has disciplined his muscles. He is a good swimmer, a passionate devotee of all winter sports. His body, consequently, moves with graceful suppleness, especially when he is playing his instrument, which in his hands is no cumbersome fellow, but seems almost like a miniature.

He has an intense face—his eyes are dark and luminous, the lines of his face are strong, and the chin is assertive. It is a photogenic face (a successful screen test was once made that brought him to the threshold of a movie career, but he vetoed the idea at the time; since then he has made a brief appearance in *Carnegie Hall*), and it has inspired several excellent paintings, one of which (by Wayman Adams) was exhibited at the Metropolitan Museum of Art and won first prize in the Carnegie Exhibit in Pittsburgh. It is a face that reflects the culture of the man: for Piatigorsky is that well-rounded type of person who refuses to make music the be-all and end-all of his intellectual existence. A mystic by nature, he is interested in all phases of philosophy. He reads voraciously, is intensely interested in politics, is a dabbler in the sciences, and writes good poetry. Beyond the pleasures of the mind, his preferences include American cigarettes, Russian food, playing cards, and indulging in practical jokes.

Since 1947, he has been an American citizen. He maintains two homes, one in Philadelphia (to be near the Curtis Institute where he is head of the 'cello department), the other a 100-acre place in Elizabethtown, New York, in the Adirondacks. His wife, formerly Jacqueline de Rothschild, daughter of Baron Edouard de Rothschild of Paris, is a good amateur musician, playing the piano and bassoon. They have two children: Jephta was born in France, and Joram in Elizabethtown.

Larry Adler

V

HARMONICA VIRTUOSO

Larry Adler

LARRY ADLER

STATISTICS inform us that one out of every thirteen people in the United States plays the harmonica. But ask professional musicians or those who know anything about the harmonica and they will insist that actually there is only one harmonica player in the world, and his name is Larry Adler.

He plays the "blues" and boogie-woogie, and the latest song hits. He also plays concertos, quartets, rhapsodies, and tone-poems, which he has arranged for his instrument. And in whatever he plays he is truly unique. He has been called the world's greatest harmonica player, the "Heifetz of the harmonica." "Sure," is Larry's comment, "there's little competition." Yet William Walton, England's celebrated composer, did not hesitate to describe Adler as a "genius."

He *is* a genius, even though his is an unorthodox musical instrument. To the harmonica, Adler brings the same equipment and native gifts that a Heifetz brings to his violin, and a Horowitz to his piano. He has that feeling for rhythm, for the phrase, for tone color, and for style which is the identifying trait of every great virtuoso. From his instrument he has learned to evoke qualities it was never before known to possess. As a critic of the New York *Times* reported: "While he seems able to do anything whatever on the instrument, including the production of remarkable color and timbre, with tones resembling the flute, the clarinet, the violin—even the muted trombone . . . it is the sheer beauty of sound that he builds up from his humble little instrument and the rhythm, phrasing, melodic line and form, as well as the fine interpretation, that capture the audience and that make him important in music."

Because of Adler, Jean Berger wrote a concerto for harmonica and orchestra; Darius Milhaud created a suite for harmonica; Cyril Scott produced the *Serenade for Larry Adler*. Because of Adler, too, symphony orchestras throughout America smashed tradition by permitting the lowly harmonica to appear as a solo instrument at regular symphony concerts.

Yet some years back, when Larry Adler applied for membership in the Musicians Union he was turned down because the Union considered the harmonica a toy and not a musical instrument. In a sense, of the many compliments paid to Adler, this is one of the highest. For it takes an inordinately great artist to take an instrument that is rejected and elevate it to the high status of artistic respectability. "The nice part of it all, and the thing I am most proud of," is Adler's comment, "is that I became so famous without once imitating a train, a freight car shunting, or those other corny tricks harmonica players do to attract attention. Why, I actually became famous because I played Vivaldi, Bach, and Mozart!"

To have raised a "toy" to the ranks of a serious musical instrument is a unique enough achievement. To have done this without being able to read a note of music puts Adler in a class by himself. The story goes that when Larry Adler was soloist with the New York Philharmonic-Symphony in the Vivaldi Concerto (originally for violin), one of the musicians in the orchestra remarked wistfully: "If he can make music *that* way without being able to read a note of music, let's all of us hurry and unlearn what we know."

Adler has been able to master a comprehensive repertoire that includes concertos, sonatas, rhapsodies, and fugues by listening to phonograph records. This method is functional for him because he has an extraordinarily sensitive ear, a remarkable memory, and an instinctive musicianship. He can listen to a large work several times and at once it is indelibly impressed on his memory as if he had learned every note from the printed page. He was once visiting a friend who played for him on records the Brahms Violin Concerto. Adler liked it, and asked to hear it again. After a second playing, the friend commented: "I wonder how it would sound on a harmonica, Larry." Unhesitatingly, Larry proceeded to show him, and played the whole thing through with only a few slips.

But there came a time when phonograph records were not enough to provide Larry with his repertoire, and that was when leading contemporary composers began writing works expressly for his use. It was then that he started learning to read music. Today he reads music fluently, and learns all his new works through the printed page. "Actually," Adler explains, "it doesn't make too much difference which way I learn my music—whether by ear or eye. The hard job for me is not in memorizing works, which has always come rather easily, but in trying to translate them for the harmonica, in trying to get over the composer's intentions as faithfully as possible on an instrument he probably never knew anything about."

To help him do this, Adler has a collection of some two hundred harmonicas of every make, size, and description. On these he experiments endlessly for different tone qual-

ities and effects. He has evolved colors and nuances through
the sweat and tears of trial and error. He has learned how
to draw from it the quality of muted strings, the plangent
tone of the oboe, the majesty of the pipe organ, the fre-
netic wails of a hot jazz band.

He gives the harmonica terrible abuse during a concert.
The legend used to circulate that Adler throws away a
harmonica after he has played a single concert. The result
has been that he has been bombarded with requests from
his admirers for his discarded instruments. The truth is
that Adler's harmonica is no longer playable, not after a
single concert, but after a few weeks.

Intimate friends of Adler are rather amused by the fact
that he is perhaps prouder of his suave and debonair manner on the concert stage than his virtuosity. He always
wears tails, and being slender and attractive, wears them
well. He feels that this brings dignity to the harmonica it
had never before possessed. He even tried to induce his
manager to change his name to "Lawrence Adler" because
he felt that the diminutive was not dignified enough for a
concert artist. "Maybe so," the manager answered, "but a
name like Jascha is also diminutive, and he seems to be
doing rather well, don't you think?" Adler never again
broached the subject.

It was his tails, as a matter of fact, that gave him his first
great opportunity in the theatre. He was scheduled to appear at the Palace Theatre in New York (a none too-well
paid, or too well-known trouper) when he decided once
and for all to make an impression. Up to then, he had always appeared on the vaudeville stage dressed as a street
urchin, smeared, dirty, ragged. The manager used to an-
nounce that he had discovered this "bootblack" or "newsboy" outside on the street. After five or six such appear-

ances, Larry grew a bit tired of both the routine and the costume. When he was engaged for the Palace Theatre, he insisted that he appear in white tie and tails.

In the audience was the famous English impresario, Charles B. Cochran. After the performance, Cochran went backstage to engage Adler for a London revue called *Streamline,* making his offer more tempting by giving Adler what was to him at the time the fabulous salary of $300 a week.

Larry Adler was naturally proud that his genius had at last been discovered. But his ego was momentarily deflated when Cochran explained: "You know, what first attracted me to you was not your playing, but the fact that a harmonica performer should be wearing white tie and tails. That, man, is showmanship!"

This was in 1934. Within a few months, Adler became the toast of London. The harmonica industry in England went into a boom because of him, the sale of the instrument suddenly soaring more than 200%. Larry Adler fan clubs were founded all over England, with a total membership of 300,000. His first recording, Jerome Kern's *Smoke Gets In Your Eyes,* sold 40,000 copies the first week. A special revue was written around him, and was produced in London; it ran more than a year. He played for the King and Queen of England, the Duke of Kent, the King of Norway. He was a guest artist at London's most exclusive night clubs, and a star on radio shows. In Monte Carlo he was paid $2,500 to give a special performance for a party for the King of Sweden.

Strange to say, Larry Adler returned from this furor abroad virtually unknown and unrecognized. He had difficulty getting an engagement in this country. It was through the ministrations of his good friend Leonard Lyons, the newspaper columnist, that he was invited to appear at

Fefe's Monte Carlo, a night club. This was so successful that Adler was engaged for the Capitol Theatre, and then at the Loew's State Theatre, both in New York City.

It was at this time that he appeared as soloist with the Chicago Women's Symphony Orchestra in a performance of a classical violin concerto which he had adapted for the harmonica. This was the first time that a harmonica became a solo instrument with a symphony orchestra. This made good copy, and the papers publicized the event. Adler's performance inspired an ovation. Other orchestral appearances followed; then recitals in concert halls in which Adler's program ran the gamut from Bach to boogie-woogie.

His concerts began to attract perhaps the most varied audiences a serious concert hall has known, ranging from the long-haired musician who came to hear Mozart and Bach to the "jive" fan. All seemed to have the time of their lives. Immediately, Adler assumed a solitary position in the world of music. He was the man who could make the "jive" fan take Mozart and draw bravos from the more serious listeners for his rendition of the "blues." He was the man who could create art with the lowly harmonica.

It was his success in the serious field that has given Adler the prominence he now enjoys, a prominence that brings him an average weekly income of $2,000. In December 1941, he began making joint appearances with the dancer Paul Draper (the man who could tap dance to the music of Lully, Bach, and other classical masters, and do it enchantingly). They became the most popular novelty act in music. A series of record breaking appearances at the Mecca Temple in New York in 1943, and repeated the next few years, netted them $7,000 a performance. Together, with the harmonica and the tap dance—and a charmingly informal way of presenting their programs—

they proved that there is actually no distinction between popular art and serious, but that there is only good art and good artists; that a great artist can play the harmonica or can tap dance and yet be as creative as his fellow-artist in the more accepted forms of artistic expression. For it is always the artist who gives his medium significance; and never vice-versa.

Larry Adler is an engaging fellow with a lovable smile and the contagiously appealing manner of the born show-man. He has a ready wit which is often engagingly spon-taneous, and he loves a good "gag." Once he was invited by Norman Corwin to appear on the radio networks in a hill-billy act. His part was that of a hill-billy who spoke in mountaineer dialect and played the harmonica. Corwin wired him to telephone him and talk "like a hill-billy," to be sure that he would do for the part. Adler followed instructions. What Corwin heard over the telephone re-ceiver was: "Deed you all veesh for me I should tuk all dis hill-billy stuff, maybe?"

He is, at other moments, a serious young man, deeply concerned over politics, and highly social-conscious. It was his deep awareness of the significance of the war that made it such a keen disappointment for him when he was turned down for the armed forces. He volunteered his harmonica instead, and made several extensive tours of the army camps in this country and of the fighting fronts. When playing for the G.I.'s, his keen democratic spirit dictated that the enlisted man should have the choice seats in prefer-ence to the high-ranking officers; he also insisted that there be no segregation between white men and black.

He lives in a luxurious apartment in New York City, with his wife, two children, a nurse, a maid, a grand piano, and his 200 harmonicas. He met his wife in London—an attractive mannequin in a West End dress shop. She has a quiet and pleasing sense of humor in her own right, and likes nothing better than to prick the bubble of her husband's vanity with well directed pin thrusts. Adler once elaborated on one of his USO trips to the Near East and described his thrilling experiences. "Imagine," he said, "I actually prayed at the Wailing Wall in Jerusalem." "What did you pray for," his wife asked, "bigger billing?"

Larry Adler was born in Baltimore on February 10, 1914. He began singing at two, heard his first concert (a recital by Rachmaninoff) at five, and at ten earned his way by singing in synagogues. He entered the Peabody School of Music to study the piano; strange to relate, he was soon dismissed because of his ineptitude for the instrument. Actually he was passionately in love with both music and the piano; and it was only the fact that he wanted (and tried) to play concertos and jazz before he had mastered the rudiments of Czerny that made him unacceptable to his teachers.

The Adlers did not have a piano in their home, and Larry set out to remedy this. He walked into one of the large music stores in Baltimore and quietly ordered a Mason and Hamlin. The salesman looked suspiciously on a boy who came to buy a $1,400 instrument, turned a deaf ear, and in place of a piano gave the boy the gift of a harmonica. Adler put the harmonica in his pocket, and still insisted that the piano be sent to his home. The story goes that his flow of rhetoric and his entreaties actually convinced the salesman to send the instrument on approval. In any case, a Mason and Hamlin *did* come into the Adler home, and it took Adler's father five years to pay off the debt.

Today Adler is quite adept at the piano. More than one

musician has heard him play and has regretted that Adler
had not taken up the study of the instrument more seriously. "If only you had!' remarked one friend wistfully.
"If only I had," answered Larry, mindful of his $100,000
a year income as harmonica virtuoso, "I'd probably be a
two-dollar-an-hour teacher in some small town."

For a period, Adler sold magazines and newspapers to
get the money for concert tickets and phonograph records.
At the same time, he began experimenting with the harmonica. In 1927, he entered a harmonica contest sponsored by the Baltimore *Sun*. He played something by
Beethoven, whereas all the others played popular songs;
and he won the first prize, a silver cup.

One year later, he came to New York—his only possessions being seven dollars in cash and his harmonica. He
haunted the offices of managers and booking agents; he
searched out the addresses of leading stage personalities
and played under their windows; he contacted stars in
their dressing rooms. "Everybody called me a genius, but
nobody would give me a job." Eventually, perseverance
won out. Playing for Rudy Vallee in his dressing room, he
was engaged by the crooner for his night club, the Heigh-
Ho. That was the beginning. He soon got a job playing
the harmonica for those Mickey Mouse cartoons in which
Mickey played that instrument. He was placed in a vaudeville unit by the orchestral maestro, Paul Ash. Then
Florence Ziegfeld engaged him for a lavish musical com-
edy, *Smiles,* which was a failure. Other stage appearances,
as well as several roles in the movies, proved that the boy
from Baltimore was getting ahead.

Then came his sensational reception in London followed by his graduation into the ranks of good music.
And Larry Adler—and the harmonica—came into their
own.